I0022316

mysteries
of yin

Man's Guide to This Beloved's Heart

J. S. Lea

Copyright © by J.S. Lea

All rights reserved. No part of this book may be reproduced or used in any manner without written permission of the copyright owner except for the use of quotations in a book review. For more information, address: J.s.lea@mysteriesofyin.com

First paperback edition August 2019

Cover design by Joshua Bruce
Illustrations by Chiaki Hagiwara

ISBN 978-1-7333685-0-6 (paperback)
ISBN 978-1-7333685-1-3 (ebook)

www.mysteriesofyin.com

Illustrations by Chiaki Hagiwara

Table of Contents

Acknowledgements

Many people are responsible for the publishing of this book. First, I would like to thank my parents and my sister, who have endured the wild adventures of a restless young boy. You have continued to support me, despite my reckless decisions and audacious voyages. Next, my beautiful wife, the love of my life. You have trusted me and followed me to the ends of the earth. Finally, my daughter, who must suffer her eccentric father through her growing years.

My sincere gratitude goes to my aunt Laura for helping me with the editing of the book, for showing me the rich flavors of the English language, and for supporting me through my years in the United States. To my aunt Aquila, who has elevated me, and shared with me her profound wisdom. To Joshua Bruce, for his brilliant cover design, to Chiaki Hagiwara for her stunning illustrations, and to Stephanie Thurwachter, for her wonderful interior design and formatting. Your artistic minds are truly beyond me.

Finally, I would like to thank all those who inspired the content of this book. The hundreds of people I met on my travels who shared with me their hearts, experiences, cultures and wisdoms. My teachers and mentors, who have steered my life in the right direction and instilled me their vast knowledge and understanding. Finally, the great masters and philosophers of human history who have graced me with their words and insights. Your imprint on my heart and soul is timeless, and I pray that my contribution can shine light on your divine impact.

The Map

Introduction

«The man who asks a question is a fool for a minute, the man who does not ask is a fool for life.»

~Confucius

An intimate relationship can be the most breathtaking adventure, infused with unending joys and granting us entries to castles in the sky. It can also shatter us beyond recognition or hope of return. So how can we navigate this most infamous riddle, this most sophisticated journey? This introduction lays out the map for our voyage ahead.

From a young age I was haunted by the question, "What is the meaning of life?" At the age of nineteen, I decided to leave the world behind and embark on a journey of discovery. My journey led me through the great castles of Europe, through the tall mountains of Asia, through the mystical islands of the Caribbean, through the vibrant cities of the western civilization, and into a vast journey through the invisible realm. I left behind my preconceived beliefs about life and the universe, and I devoted myself to the pursuit of this one question. Like Michelangelo carving out his angel in the marble, I gradually stripped off layers of my perceptions, dogmas, and beliefs, until only one principle remained in my sight. When all my filters were dismantled it shined through like a beacon: "Taiji", the ancient divine principle.

It appeared to me that every process in our universe is governed by Taiji, the cosmic fusion between Yin & Yang. The very fabric of our physical universe is constructed, sustained and perpetuated by the masculine and feminine interactions within the nuclei of an atom. Furthermore, life, and all physical processes are continued and multiplied by the interplay of Yin & Yang. Protons & electrons in the particle kingdom, stamen & pistil in the plant kingdom, male & female in the animal kingdom, and man & woman in our kingdom, are all symbols of this all-embracing principle that makes life possible. The fulfilment of this principle, I discovered, was indeed the purpose of life.

As a man, the pursuit and discovery of Yin, the feminine principle, became my central ambition. I discovered that it's within the relationship with a woman, that a man finds his ultimate purpose. I continued my travels and search for answers. I met with people from all corners of the world. I listened to their stories, and absorbed their cultures, experiences, wisdoms and beliefs. I studied nature and immersed myself in the teachings of great spiritual masters and philosophers. I meditated, I contemplated, I fasted, and I traveled into the far edges of the spiritual realms. Finally, a vast ocean of insights poured over me. It felts as if I asked for a cup of water but was launched into the Pacific Ocean. At last I discovered some simple secrets, like buried treasures, and I have attempted to reconstruct the path that led me to these insights.

This book is purposed to be a map, designed to facilitate the journey ahead. Beware, it includes some intricate drawings, and it will guide you through some narrow passages and over some steep, treacherous trails. Be patient as we navigate through unfamiliar lands and triumph over unforgiving terrain. We will explore four highly distinct sections. Each section will reveal a new layer of understanding and mirror the journey I went through.

To love well, we must first be strong and mature, able to appreciate, support and protect our beloved. The first section of this book, *Pathway to Perfection,* is dedicated to helping you develop these inherent qualities. First, you need to know in your bones, your true value as a person and as a man. Armed with this knowledge, you will be able to break free from the restraints that may have bound you to failure in the past. Next, you will need to find your passion in life, and develop the maturity and leadership qualities necessary to sustain you in your path. Through the first three chapters, you will develop the confidence, insight and strength to overcome the many challenges imbued in an intimate relationship.

Chapters 4, 5 and 6 make up the section: *Pathway to Women*. They will give you a window into the mysterious inner workings of the mind and heart of a woman. To my surprise, a woman is not really that complicated. Once you discover the secrets to her yearnings and needs, you will be able to lead her in the euphoric dance of love. In this section we will discover the true meaning of harmony and beauty, and we will learn to satisfy the deep inner yearnings of a woman.

These topics are crucial to a successful relationship. However, there is a more elusive truth that defines the quality of our interactions. The third section of this book, *Pathway to Energy*, dives into the invisible realm, explores the infinite expressions and dimensions of love, and teaches you how to master the great force of Taiji together with your girl. It offers a revolutionary perspective into the hidden forces that drive our interactions and will allow you to access uncharted realms of intimacy and connectedness.

The final section of this book, *Pathway to Mastery*, provides specific techniques and methods to help you apply the insights you have gained through the other sections. Each chapter corresponds to the previous three sections, respectively. We will look at tools to develop the self-mastery we need to advance along our chosen path, we will explore non-verbal and verbal ways to communicate intimacy, and finally, we will learn about universal nutrition, the fuel that enable us to actualize our potentials.

We will never completely fulfill our potential to love, because our capacity is infinite. If this statement sounds foreign to you now, you will come to see the truth of it by the end of this book. I hope you will enjoy your reading, and that through these stories you will be surprised by deep, life-changing insights. Through my travels, I gained an unexpected joy, and I felt compelled to share it with you. This book is a milestone for me in my journey, and I hope it is for you in yours as well. It is my deepest hope that you will succeed in your love-life, and that you will live in abundant joy with your sweetheart.

Yours sincerely,
J.S. Lea

Pathway to Perfection

Section 1

Section I is founded on the belief that success in a relationship, and in life, is a product of self-mastery. Through this section we will seek to resolve our inner conflicts, discover our higher calling, and develop the skills and qualities of true leadership.

Journey to Freedom

Chapter 1

«Your task is not to seek for love, but to find all the barriers within yourself that you have built against it.»

~Rumi

Freedom. What a stunning word, if we stop to ponder it for a moment. Freedom from constraints, from limitations, from chains that bind us to an undesirable fate. Freedom to explore, to invent, and to unravel all the magical mysteries this universe has to offer. The most astounding mystery, of course, at least according to Steven Hawking, is *woman.* Hence our title, *Mysteries of Yin.* Yin is a term used in Chinese classical philosophy for the feminine principle, inherent to the duality of the Tao. Masculine and feminine energies exist in a dynamic relationship as complementary partners necessary to bring about this universe. Necessary to bring about you and me. And necessary for us to discover and rejoice.

So, where do we begin? I hope you read the introduction. I made it short on purpose so you would. It provides the map for our journey ahead. But now it's time for us to begin. Let's start with ourselves, as men. This first chapter will help you start your quest to discover your true manhood and to build the foundation you need to succeed as a lover. Yes, let us begin.

The Three Great Blessings

At the dawn of human history, man was granted three great blessings: to become fruitful, to multiply and to have dominion over all things. Like a tree reaching maturity and the ability to produce fruits, being fruitful means to fulfill our potentials, reach maturity, and obtain individual perfection. To multiply means to perpetuate life, which is a fruit of the perfect bond with a woman. Finally, to have dominion means to become masters over the natural world. Sounds astonishing, doesn't it? Why is it that after all these millennia, we still haven't gotten there? Somehow our social fabric has created a barrier for us to reach our potential as men, and as a result, the remaining two blessings have been cut off from our reach. The purpose of this chapter is to overcome our personal limitations so to free us to fulfill the three great blessings.

A man in love is like a charming prince embarking on a conquest of a foreign land. He approaches his princess with his heart in his hand, and all his strengths and virtues at her command. But unfortunately, he also comes to her with his weaknesses, personal challenges, and irrational behaviors. As they grow more intimate, these problems are no longer his own; they become an engraved part of their relationship. For these reasons, before you conquer your princess, you must conquer yourself: overcome your personal limitations, and cultivate your emotional, mental and physical maturity.

Our beliefs may seem harmless because they're abstract and invisible, and besides, everyone's entitled to their beliefs. But beliefs affect perception and emotion and drive us to action. They shape character development and even personality. False and self-limiting beliefs are the root of what holds us back in life, they are the ropes that bind us to a limiting self-image and a lesser future. Since our personal constraints harm us in so many ways, our first order of business is to break their hold.

Strengthen your Chain

There's wonderful wisdom in the saying that the strength of a chain is only as great as its weakest link. A chain with a weak link will break, because that link compromises the entire chain. Repairing the weak link will help us uncover the true strength of the chain. If we have an irrational fear or emotional wound, then this constraint colors our entire experience of life. It blinds us to our potential and to the abundant opportunity and exquisite beauty that greet us daily. Before we can repair our weak links, we must recognize where they are and how they got there.

The primary focus of this first chapter is to expand our awareness, because it's truly the key to evolution. Everyone faces their own unique constraints, and if we search our minds ardently, free from fear and pride, we can uncover the keys to our personal evolution. Be excited to unearth these hidden constraints, because awareness is a powerful catalyst for change. In Chapter 10 we will revisit the topic of constraints and offer strategies to break them, but for now awareness will be our goal. The first question to ask is, "What are my constraints?"

If you are not exactly where you want to be, why is that? What is it that you want to do, but can't? What are you trying to hide, what's your excuse, and what are you afraid of? Is there a story you play over and over in your mind that keeps you from moving on? Why is your relationship not working the way you want it to?

Become accustomed to asking these questions, and over time, answers will come to you. Don't judge yourself. Instead enjoy the relief of finally hunting down the lies that have plagued you, and of bringing them out of the deep recesses of your mind. A particularly effective method is to ask your friends for their insights. Ask them to truthfully reveal things they appreciate about you, and things you could improve on. The ability to see yourself with the eyes of others is a life-changing gift. Be excited to discover your flaws and false beliefs, and trust that as you come to know yourself better, you will become free to enjoy your life and fulfill your potential.

The courage to look at yourself honestly and to confront your failings is quite rare. Our sky-high divorce rate and the fact that domestic violence is common indicate that people usually don't want to admit their problems. I admire any man who has the sincerity and wisdom to look for ways to improve his love life. In our world, people can obtain master's degrees in economics, engineering, mathematics or phycology, but strangely there is no way to graduate from the school of love. Oddly, people believe that they will succeed without making much effort. Why do we believe that love is easy? Because it looks like so much fun? Of course, it should be fun, but as we have said before, it requires us to be reasonably free of personal limitations. Let's look at some common problems, recognize some of the lies behind them, and consider some higher perspectives. We will start with 3 common challenges that many men struggle with.

1) A Destructive Self- Image

Many people suffer from a poor self-image. Insecurities cause them to keep their distance from others, and so their partners often feel ignored. Where does true confidence come from? Some people believe that being good-looking is the key to confidence, so they go to the gym to lift weights. Others believe that having a lot of money will make them confident, so they go to the stock market. They believe that once they get that body, that car, that college degree, or that perfect girl, then they will become confident. Unfortunately, it rarely works that way.

There is nothing wrong with pursuing these things, but don't be fooled into believing they will bring you confidence or happiness. In fact, often these things have the opposite effect. When we keep telling ourselves we need this and that to be happy or confident, we end up convincing ourselves. We train our minds into believing that happiness and confidence only exists in the obtainment of our next exterior pursuit. Thus, we pursue it to the ends of the Earth, like a horse chasing its carrot. Of course, in the end it can't satisfy us, because confidence and happiness can't come from outside ourselves. They come from within, from our mindsets and our beliefs.

Gaining self-confidence is much easier than people think, it has to do with consistently acting in a way worthy of respect. If your thoughts and actions consistently inspire your higher conscience, you will naturally begin to think more highly of yourself. That said, we tend to become overly critical of ourselves as we grow up. Therefore, we should reconnect with our childhood confidence, and remember that it's engraved in our DNA to value and love ourselves.

Think of how kids are usually bursting with confidence. They see the world as their oyster, as their playground, and each one of them knows they're the best singer, the fastest runner and the most talented painter in the world! It doesn't matter whether their perceptions are true, because these beliefs give them the joy and the freedom to grow. And of course, young children have zero inhibitions and have never met any person who isn't a friend. I can still remember my worldviews as a child. I remember seeing a cute girl sitting by the swing, never worrying whether she would like me. I would just run up and play with her, to find out if she was as awesome as I was! Either that or I'd pour a cup of water over her head to get her attention!

At some point, however, something changes. One day we look at someone else's painting and realize that maybe we aren't as great as we thought. This is a decisive moment in a kid's life. One kid says, "Cool, there's someone who can teach me to become even *more* awesome!" The other kid says, "Oh, whatever, what's the point. I suck at everything." For the second kid, the problem is not the realization that he's not perfect, but that he focuses on his insufficiency rather than the opportunity to grow.

Self-abasement is perhaps the most widespread form of self-deception and is surely one of the greatest impediments preventing men from enjoying life and from freely loving their woman. They lose touch with their inner greatness, and they cling to beliefs that don't serve them. Over time these beliefs harden into bad habits and negative personality traits. For this reason, it's vital that we learn to love ourselves, to accept ourselves, and to realize our inherent internal qualities.

It doesn't help anyone if you have the unrealistic expectation that you will be the first perfect man. You can choose to make peace with yourself as you are, with all your strengths, weaknesses and unique qualities. To say that a woman wants a confident man is very different from saying that she wants a perfect man. It's the combination of strength and vulnerability, of what we offer and what we need, of what is mature in us and what is just being born, that makes us fascinating to each other. Authenticity is what a woman is seeking, and this is what we are failing to give her. It is for us to cultivate self-confidence, meaning self-acceptance and transparency.

2) Sex: An Ancient and Poetic Mystery

A multitude of mental and emotional issues are derived from a misguided understanding of sexuality, yet it holds the very key to our ultimate freedom. People have been obsessed with sex since ancient times. It is not a new phenomenon. The ancient Greeks believed that the climax was the most profound way to unite with the gods. The odd thing is that even though we are so obsessed, we are oblivious to its true meaning and significance. Of course, we know the obvious, but there are so many problems stemming from our ignorance of its true origin. Somehow all that obsession over the centuries hasn't helped us much.

Confusion about sex in our day is amplified by the media. We are inundated with sexual images, fantasies, and even sexual violence through music, movies, and the internet. Some of what we see is heartless, mindless animalism, and some of what we see is sugar-coated fantasy. But very little of it offers valuable insight. We are robbed from any valuable education because our parents and our teachers are too ashamed to talk about it, and those who do talk about it, shout it from the mountaintops in the light of rebellion and debauchery.

Decent people don't talk about sex because of our misguided view of purity, often promoted by religion. Many of us believe that anything having to do with physical desire, especially sexual desire, is inherently impure. Hence the idea that conception without intercourse is "immaculate." Since we can't perpetuate human life without sex, I wonder whether some people believe that God is playing tricks on us. I wonder if they consider what would happen if everyone became celibate to honor Him. Let's stop to think for a moment about the importance that sexuality has to life, about the overarching duality of Yin & Yang, the positive and negative polarity that permeates the universe and all energies; the very foundation for our existence. We must embrace an understanding of nobility and purity that can exalt our sexual nature, rather than deny it, otherwise we will continue to perpetuate a destructive sexual paradigm.

Human sexuality is not merely about satisfying physical and emotional cravings, it is part of a cosmic phenomenon that defines and sustains our universe. Yin & Yang are the two founding principles that upholds the cosmos, and their interaction is the defining dynamic that perpetuates life. The ongoing dance between electrons and protons is the building block for the entire physical world, and it symbolizes the masculine and feminine interplay. Courtships between male and female animals, and between the masculine and feminine characteristics of plants (stamen and pistil), are the rituals that multiply life. The Big Bang that instigated the creation of all things was nothing less than a cosmic climax between the two principles. We must learn to see our sexual natures as part of the founding principles of our universe, and recognize it as the strongest, most beautiful and most essential force of the human spirit.

Because sexual energy is a constant presence flowing through our veins, it's central to our identity. Your sexual activities give shape and color to the energy that moves through your mind, body and soul. It becomes a part of who you are. If you seek to gain physical pleasure only, then it blinds you to the higher and original qualities that sexual energy represents. Sexual energy has a supreme and special purpose, and casual use will not only blind you to its deeper meaning, but ultimately lead to your demise. If, on the other hand, you harmonize your sexuality with the universal energies that make the sun rise and set, then it will grant you with health and vitality. It will become your closest experience of the primordial life force itself.

We will discuss more practical applications of this during this book, but for now it's important to recognize sex as a divine gift, a celebration of love, and a sublime nourishment of our souls. Euphoric love happens when we are not consumed by our own needs, but rather enraptured in the moment, and connected to a higher ideal. Only in this context can we experience what sex is all about – a divine celebration of the cosmic intelligence.

3) The Deceptive Lower Nature

Tom & Jerry had it right. Our inner dialogue can often be depicted by an angel and a devil on our shoulders. We all face an internal conflict between our higher and lower natures. This conflict stands as one of the greatest mysteries of the human condition. Psychologists might call our lower nature "the ego" and theologians might call it as our "sinful nature." J.R.R Tolkien personified it as Gollum. Whatever we call it, our lower nature exists as the dark force that splits our soul into contradictory desires.

The more we're aware of this, the more we can purify and vivify our interactions and our experiences of life.

You've probably noticed that some days you feel off, and other days you feel clear and empowered. This is determined by which of your two natures is dominant. Our lower nature is our inferior self. We recognize it in the times we hate, when we know we should forgive, when we are self-righteous even though our conscience begs us to be humble, and when we choose ignorance when we could open our minds to greater truths. Most people also recognize their higher nature. It's expressed when we help someone who may not deserve it, and when we choose to listen even though we're certain we're right. We access our higher selves when we decide to work on our deficiencies or accept a challenge that seems beyond us. At these times, we discover our inner strength and inherent glory.

Our higher self is our original self. It's who we truly are. Our lower self is a self-deception. It's a great mystery that we often choose to listen to the voice of our lower nature, even though we know deep inside the damages and hurts it inflicts on ourselves and the people we love. We must recognize the lower nature as a highly seductive and powerful force.

We all have a lower nature. There is nothing we can do about that. However, we can decide which part of ourselves to identify with, and which words we accept as our truth. The mastery of this dynamic is indeed the path to perfection. The way to overcome our lower nature is to recognize it and render it impotent by choosing our higher nature as our guide. We will discover methods to do this throughout the book, but first let's look at how our lower nature deceives us.

The Two Wolves

According to an ancient native American saying, we all have two wolves inside of us, constantly fighting. The one that wins, is whichever we feed the most. Likewise, there are two voices in our minds: one that speaks wisdom and encouragement, and another that speaks deception and is bent on our self-destruction. Whichever we choose to listen to, will shape our destiny.

To understand how the lower nature works, picture yourself going to a job interview. You are well prepared, and you know that you are a good candidate. However, as you walk into the waiting room, a strange voice seeps into your mind. It tells you that you're not good enough, that they will never hire someone like you, or that it's not even worth applying. This voice belongs to your lower nature. In these moments it is crucial to reboot, to connect with your higher self, and to go forward anyway. If you don't, your lower self will often win you over with surprisingly persuasive reasoning.

Your lower nature uses many devious arguments to confound your mind. It will tell you confidently that what you have done so far has kept you safe, so you should never venture beyond your comfort zone. It might give you stern warning that you're about to make a fool of yourself in front of your friends. It reminds you that no one likes you, so it's best to blend into the scenery. And it tries to convince you that you will most likely fail, so it's better to save your energy. It can also tell you that people are ignorant, so you should not listen to them, or that it's better to put them in their place than to be humble. Based on these arguments, our lower nature keeps us from living freely, it keeps us from connecting with people or from learning new things, and it keeps us from seeing all the exciting opportunities that life provides.

Let's briefly look at a few more characteristics of our lower nature so that we can discover the warning signs of its influence and gain mastery of our inner dialogue.

Fear that Binds Us

Your lower nature may place irrational restrictions on you that hinder you from living the life you truly want. Perhaps you really enjoy collecting stamps, but of course you can't do that. Or can you? Perhaps you want to talk to the person sitting next to you at the bus stop, but you couldn't. Or could you? Perhaps you want to call your sweetheart while you wait in line at the grocery store, just to tell her how much you adore her, but … Personally I don't see any reason why you can't do these things, but your lower nature infuses your mind with the fear that other people might disapprove of you, and so your fear controls you. If you wonder in what ways this is true for your life, ask yourself the question: "If no one was there to see it, would my life be any different?" Now, free yourself to live in alignment with your true self. Your opinion is the one that matters.

Self-approval, based on a sense of peace with your own higher nature, is what you're after. All the rest is details.

The Proverbial Elephant

Hindus tell the story of the Proverbial Elephant. It's about four blind men who are brought into a courtyard to describe an elephant. One of them describes a column, like a tree. Another discovers something flat and flexible like a curtain. A third encounters a sharp spear, and the fourth man describes a thick rope. Each of them is certain of what he has found, because after all, he has touched the great pillar, he has bent the flat sheet, he was pierced by the sharp spear, or he has tested the strong rope. Each is certain that the others are deceived! But a seeing man would know at once that they have all touched an elephant there in the courtyard. Each of the men are correct. They possess a fragment of the truth. But it is only by integrating their views and reaching a common understanding that they can unveil the reality.

The men of the story are physically blind, but more to the point, they are bound by the impulse to cling to their convictions, regardless of what other people might have experienced, or what others might have to say. When Jesus told his disciples, "I have much more to say to you... I have spoken to you in figures, but a time will come for me to speak plainly," his disciples responded, "Now you are speaking plainly." Even though they believed He was the voice of God, they could not fathom that He had more to tell them.

Our lower nature is a powerful force that keeps us from entertaining new ideas. It convinces us that our limited experience of life is sufficient, and that the opinions of others are either not valid or not useful. It's the reason why we have thousands of religious denominations despite 70% of their content being identical.

Have you ever asked yourself why you are hesitant to opening your mind when listening to a perspective that differs from your own? We all know that listening well and learning an alternative view can only enhance our understanding. The logic of our higher self cannot find any reason for our hesitation, but our lower nature controls us even so. It's up to us to stop ourselves when we get into a closed state of mind, and follow our true heart and the promptings of our higher nature.

Irrational Waves of Emotion

Another aspect of our lower nature causes us to be overwhelmed by negative emotions. We may feel great frustration and anger over insignificant things, or we might lose it for no reason whatsoever. The most trivial things such as getting cut off in traffic or having to wait in a long line at the mall can cause us to lose composure. Later we might feel stupid for reacting that way, but the damage is already done. Other times we are not even aware of how out of control we are. We just act the way we feel, without stopping to think about why we feel the way we do, and whether or not our feelings make sense. The anger, frustration, or other negative emotions which rise up in these situations does not stem from our original heart. They rise from our lower nature, which is not our true and eternal self. It's important that we are careful about allowing these feelings to influence our behavior.

**

Balancing the conflicting forces within ourselves requires a healthy dose of wisdom and self-mastery. When we are in an intimate relationship this dynamic becomes even more complicated, because within every interaction there are conflicting forces of higher and lower natures influencing every word and action. Rather than studying solutions to every conflict that may arise in a relationship, we should practice our awareness of the contradictory forces within us. If we can recognize the influence of our lower self, and render it impotent by accessing our higher self, we can unveil hidden resources and resolve the majority of conflicts that arise in our relationships and in our personal lives.

The lower nature is deeply rooted in us. We might not be able to completely dispel it, but we can master it. First, we must choose to identify with our higher selves. Then we can speak to our lower selves as we would speak to a child. Remember, you don't fight with a five-year-old, but you don't follow his advice about the stock market, either. When irrational fears or lower impulses arise in your throat, speak to it as if it had a personality and a thought process of its own. Tell it, "I know you are frightened and worried, and I know that we are outside our comfort zone. Don't worry. I promise to take care of us."

Awareness is the greatest medicine. When we are aware, we are automatically drawn to solutions. Later in this book, particularly in Chapter 10, we will look more into techniques to help us rise above our lower nature and draw on our many inner resources. For now, suffice it to say that with consistent efforts, you can free yourself from many of the fears, angers, and other harmful emotions that you may struggle with today.

Two Common Mistakes

I will not go too deeply into how to cure our constraints at this point, because I believe that awareness alone is a powerful catalyst for change. Also, it is important to develop the maturity to look at our own challenges and deal with them in the manner appropriate to our situation. However, I wanted to warn you against the feelings of despair that might arise as we work on healing our flaws. We all wish we were perfect, strong, rich, intelligent, famously talented, and stunningly handsome. But the fact is, transformation takes time. So, remember to go easy on yourself. We all have a few steps to walk before achieving our cherished dreams. Forgive yourself and trust in your journey.

I'd like to shed light on two common traps that many people fall into when they first become aware of their hidden limitations. The first is the temptation to look for a quick fix. We wish for that one technique or "magic pill" to transform our relationship into a fairy tale of wonderment, and our lives into a living dream. Unfortunately, you will be disappointed. Quick fixes might get you through a crisis, just like duct tape will keep your muffler secured for a few miles. The quick fix approach is destructive not only because it's ineffective, but also because it distracts you and keeps you from dealing with the real issues at hand. If you fail to deal with the essential issues behind your difficulty, then just wait a few days. There seems to be a universal law that right around the corner from our encounters with our own failings, we stumble into yet another disaster, all because we didn't see the previous challenge as an opportunity to grow. Whatever your challenge may be, it is given to you for a reason. Why not honor the experience by exploring it and by meeting it well?

A second mistake people make when they discover an internal constraint is that they declare war against their weaknesses or bad habits. When we become too absorbed with the problem at hand, we become blinded to the inner resources at our disposal. Instead of attacking our weaknesses, we should consciously make efforts to develop the functions of the spirit, our intellect, willpower and heart. When we have developed our internal qualities, the challenges ahead seem infinitely smaller. Going to war against our challenges, bombarding ourselves with radical remedies and powerful treatments will seldom get us anywhere. This is because anything we try to fight responds by resisting, and anything we try to hide manifests on a deeper level, or in a different context. The way to overcome our internal and external challenges is to become aware of them, make peace with them, educate ourselves, and act constructively.

Closing Thoughts

Dealing with our internal constraints is perhaps the most difficult part of self-improvement, and I applaud your willingness to face yourself and work toward becoming a better man. During this book we will explore many interesting questions related to the pursuit of your girl. However, the foundation of your success in building a great love-relationship depends on your character traits, habits, and views of the world. Hopefully, this first chapter has given you a place to start. As you already know, you begin by resolving your constraints. It gets much easier to do this once you start to view obstacles and limitations as steppingstones and a necessary part of your evolution. Ultimately our goal is not to be free from challenges but to become strong enough to handle them. Take time to reflect and discover the areas you struggle with, and during this book you will discover insights on how to deal with them.

Awareness alone is a surprisingly powerful medicine. Once we gain full awareness of a new constraint, its origin and its substance, our subconscious begins to work to restore balance. Either it can solve your challenges immediately as realizations change your view of the world, or it can bring to light a pathway to healing. Therefore, it is essential to educate ourselves. Study, seek, and learn from great teachers and philosophers, investigate your own experiences and explore the far corners of the world.

New awareness brings light to new paradigms and perspectives and it is truly the healthiest and the most effective way to broaden our minds and cure our constraints.

Discover your Calling

Chapter 2

«The two most important days of a man's life is the day he is born, and the day he finds out why»

~ Mark Twain (Apocryphal)

We are not on this earth without reason; each of us is born with a divine calling, an aspiration that beckons to us from deep within. It's a defining moment in a man's life when he discovers his calling and dedicates himself to its fulfillment. Suddenly he is not just drifting along, unable to make out meaning from his existence. He lives for his cause, his vision, his dream.

A woman wants to be taken on an adventure. She yearns to climb aboard her man's ship and sail towards the horizon. To sail of on your voyage, you must have a direction and a purpose. For a woman it matters little where you are on this journey, or even where you're going. It's your clarity and drive that speaks to her, the excitement and joy you experience as your personal quest unfolds.

How do we find that purpose that will stir our souls and ignite the flame of true ambition? And once we find it, how do we move towards it?

The purpose of this chapter is to discover our true calling, and to set sail towards its fulfilment.

Setting Your Course

When hiking the trail of destiny, the path ahead can seem treacherous, intimidating and overwhelming. This perception leads many to give up their dreams before they've even begun to climb. I'm here to encourage you that the difference between the path leading to failure and the path leading to success is often so minute as to be imperceptible. What separates success from failure is often in the smallest of details.

Tony Robbins uses the metaphor of driving a golf ball towards a four-hundred-yard hole. If you think only about where the ball lands, you would say that there is a huge difference in a shot that hits the green and one that puts the ball in water or sand. You would never imagine that the difference in the two strokes is determined by no more than a few millimeters in the point of impact of the club against the ball. Separation between success and failure is often a matter of small details. The key to success lies in our ability to recognize and control the determining factors, even if they seem insignificant at first glance.

The first thing to be aware of when striking a golf ball is the point of impact and the angle of the stroke; as we pursue our dreams, we must discover the right direction to take. So how do we choose? And what do we do to move toward our objective effectively? We must understand the fine art of goalsetting.

In this chapter, we will discuss the methods of self-discovery that enable you to discover and actualize your goals in life. But first, I'd like to introduce you to some techniques of goal-setting that will take your ambitions out of the realm of dreams and into a vivid and present interplay with your daily life. I want you to know that your goals are attainable, and that your dreams are the precursor to a better life.

A Technique for Setting Goals

A universally recognized technique that dramatically increases your ability to accomplish your objectives is to write down clearly defined goals. This is widely understood across many areas of application. Schools tell kids to do it, businesses require executives to do it, and coaches push their athletes to do it. Make your goals clear in your mind, write them down on paper. If you do this, then your goals will become emblazoned in your consciousness.

When you put your goals foremost in your mind it drives opportunities and possibilities to unfold. This phenomenon can be explained by the Reticular Activating System (RAS) Theory. The RAS is a structure within your brain that filters out irrelevant stimulation and draws out and highlights whatever is familiar or important. Because of this system, if we're focused on failure, then we will see the signs of imminent doom all around, and failure is what we will create. If we focus on our vision of success, then we will discover opportunities along our way and gain the buoyancy of spirt to take advantage of them.

Recall the last time you bought a new jacket, or a friend bought a new car. Do you remember suddenly seeing that exact same car, everywhere? The reason is that this specific car or jacket has become familiar to you, and so you notice it everywhere. Your brain filters out all the thousands of cars that pass you on the highway, until suddenly you see that one car that's familiar to you. The same thing happens when you focus on what you wish to achieve. If you focus on a certain goal, opportunities to fulfill that goal will begin to reveal themselves to you.

A clear and vivid goal is the first of *three* elements that enable a man to fulfill his calling. Your personal commitment is the *second* component. You will need to assess the level of investment you are willing to devote to the attainment of your goal, because part of a successful plan includes your taking responsibility to invest the required time, money and effort to bring your dreams to fruition. *Finally,* your success depends on your ability to break your internal constraints and restraining habits, and to let go of whatever holds you back. Let's examine these three essential questions: "What do I want?", "What am I willing to invest?" and "What am I willing to renounce?"

1) What Do I Want?

To discover your purpose, you need to spend time in meditation;

you need to look within and listen for the quiet voice of your heart. You will soon realize that satisfying goals don't have to be as flamboyant as pursuing an Olympic medal or the cure for cancer, although they could be. An honorable objective may be huge, but it could be simple. Your objectives are glorious if they ring true to you.

Be aware that sustainable goals include aspects that nourish ourselves, as well as aspects that benefit others. You can see this balance in nature. Within our solar system, for example, each planet rotates on its own axis *and* around the sun. This principle is engraved in nature: the purpose of each entity must satisfy the purpose of the whole, and the purpose of the whole must satisfy the purpose of the individual. In the same way, we need to experience personal satisfaction and contribute to a public ideal. In other words, if you only think about your own needs, you will feel empty no matter what you achieve. On the other hand, if you deny all personal desire, you will lose motivation and eventually run out of power. The solution is to recognize both your individual needs and your higher calling. Once you harmonize these two aspects of purpose, you will tap into the internal and external support you need to reach your goals.

To achieve this harmony, however, you must spend time every day considering your values, priorities and goals. This self-awareness will give you a new outlook on life. The rich value of your life will begin to dawn on you, and you will become conscious of the profound consequences of your choices. You will discover the surprising fact that getting what you want is often not nearly as challenging as figuring out what you want.

I recommend a daily morning ritual, ideally as the first thing you do when you wake up, before breakfast, before you brush your teeth, preferably before you get out of bed. Take the first unspoiled moment of the day, when your mind is clear and free of distraction.

The Morning Ritual

You have but one moment, which is of course, now. In the same way, you have but one day. This one day encompasses all aspects of your life: your joys, challenges, routines, and chance encounters. In this moment, in this day, you are creating a model for your whole life. As this day goes, so likely will go tomorrow, and many days to come. So, begin this precious day with a promise to yourself that you will be intentional.

Let the morning open with your decision to create a memorable day rich with meaning. Focus on what is important to you and determine to maintain that focus throughout the day.

People fail to pursue greatness not from lack of will, or even from self-doubt, but because of a blindness to their true purpose. Very often we don't know what we want. As a result, we float along, struggling mindlessly through each day. In order to live well we must live intentionally and in accordance with our principles and goals. The first step is to get in touch with your core desires. Often, our true desires lie dormant within us, because we just don't take time for them. We are too busy bringing home that paycheck, studying for that final, watching that football game, that we lose touch of our purpose. The first step to clarity of purpose is to hear the voice of our true aspirations, and then take all the information that it tells us and refine it.

Each morning I create a list of everything I wish I could have, or do, or be. Over time, I synthesize these ideas, and thus discover what is truly important to me. The morning ritual I will share with you is my tool to uncover my true calling. It gives me clarity, and through it I can bring the details of my day into resonance with my higher ideal.

Every morning, follow these three steps:

Step 1) Ask Yourself the Question; "What do I want?"

Answer this question with your intuitive heart. Free your imagination, listen to your higher self, and write down everything you wish for, everything you would like to be, and everything you would do if restrictions didn't apply. Your list could include physical, spiritual, emotional or mental aspirations. Get a leather-bound journal, and a fountain pen, because elegance and quality express your commitment to and faith in yourself, and they give you the feel of something fresh on the horizon. Most importantly, it looks better.

Your list may include abstract items, like happiness, or something concrete like a career advancement. It might be something physical like overcoming an illness or getting fit, or it might involve becoming more comfortable around strangers. You may want to develop a virtue, or help a friend conquer a challenge, or even indulge in an adventure. It doesn't matter. Remember it's your list. Also, try not to worry at this point about the "how." Instead focus on the "what", discover the "why", and inevitably the "how" will unveil before you.

Whatever comes up during this precious time each day should be kept sacred, so don't judge or filter the thoughts that come to mind. Also, no need to share the list with others, instead, let your accomplishments speak for themselves. Some things might seem selfish. I sometimes find myself writing stuff in the category of a new car or a trip to Hawaii, but that's OK. As you spend time doing this every day you will eventually discover patterns revealing what's truly important to you. Don't be afraid to change your list. If you keep an open mind, you will gradually strip away layer after layer, until you eventually discover the essence of what you want. That is your calling in life, at least for the time being.

Step 2) Affirm Your List Through Visualization

Once you have defined your direction and determined your goals, the next step is to harness the power of your subconscious mind in bringing them to fruition. The RAS's ability to glean familiar and important information is only one of your mind's remarkable powers. Many recent studies document the surprising effectiveness of visualization. This technique is at the heart of the daily ritual. Mastery of the subtle keys inherent to this technique makes the difference between landing a hole in one or landing in the sand.

The art of visualization can be learned. The goal is to bring into play as many of your five senses as possible, not just your sight. Each of your senses should be engaged and introduced to your list. Visualization is most effective when you create vivid multi-sensory reveries, like memories, which resonate with and become part of your life experience.

In order to introduce your senses to your desires, vividly imagine the experiences you would like to have. If you want to learn to play the guitar, imagine holding a guitar, feeling its weight, and strumming your fingers against the strings. Smell the atmosphere, the warm scent of the wooden body and the metal strings. Listen to the music you are playing and let it ring in your ears until it forms a strong impression in your mind. Feel your fingers move in harmony with the music. If this moment had a taste, what would it taste like? Make this as real as possible by engaging each of your senses in the experience.

If you want to inherit a virtue, spend time meditating on it. For instance, if you are looking for more confidence, breathe in the air of confidence, feel how it flows through your body. Notice how your confidence changes your perception. Notice changes in the colors around you, and whether the textures become clearer. Notice that your body feels different. Perhaps it is more balanced, lighter, or stronger, and notice your body language in your mind's eye. Visualize how you would handle situations differently, with ease, joy and strength. Feel how other people respond to you differently. Make your imaginings as real as possible.

What you create in your mind works as a seed that can bear fruit in actual, physical events. Meditation and visualization are therefore profoundly effective tools. Your thoughts shape your mind, your belief system, your outlook on life, as well as your direction. If you spend time meditating on a virtue or ability, you will find that quality coming more naturally to you over time, and if you visualize where you want to go in life, you will find yourself heading in that direction.

Step 3) Breathe and Believe

You have set your goals and made the first step to achieving them by focusing your mind, setting your determination, and visualizing your success. Now take a moment to allow this vivid experience to settle in your soul. Allow the flush of excitement to stir in your body as you prepare to meet a new day, laden with opportunity and imbued with the rich undercurrents of joy. Do not become impatient or unsettled; just breathe, deeply, slowly and intentionally. Believe in your own abilities, and in the cosmic powers and principles available to support those with noble ambitions. Smile to the universe and get ready for a new day.

2) What am I Willing to Invest?

A young man once attended a concert featuring his favorite pianist. As the maestro began to play, the youth was stunned by the beauty of the sounds. The warmth, passion and power of the music swept the entire hall into ecstasy. After the concert, the young man approached the virtuoso and cried, "I would do *anything* to play the way you do!" The Pianist looked at him with sincere and gentle eyes, and said simply, "You think you would, but no, my friend, no indeed, you wouldn't..."

It's not enough to wish for the universe, or God, to grant your desires. You must invest something. If you want to become a professional musician, you will have to put in at least ten thousand hours of practice. This is not a bad thing. It is part of the fun! But if you are not willing to do that, you do not want it enough. And that's OK. It's just that there are other things more important to you in life. The purpose of this chapter is to discover that purpose that sparks your desire to devote yourself wholeheartedly.

We tend to look at great intellectual or athletic icons like Einstein and Schwarzenegger, thinking they were born with bigger brains or stronger muscles. We ignore to see the process that brought them to their apex. They were undoubtedly gifted as youths, but what set Albert and Arnold apart is that they were obsessed with their fields of interest, and relentless in the pursuit of their goals. Great people are not simply born into this world different from the rest of us. While it's true that some people are born with latent talents, those who make history are those fiercely dedicated to their disciplines. So, the question we must ask ourselves is: "What are we willing to invest?"

If you want to learn to play the piano, how much time are you willing to invest? An hour a week, an hour a day, or perhaps eighteen hours a day? Determine to be consistent and to give what you honestly wish to give. You may find that the investment required to hit your target is too much or too little. Be flexible and adjust your commitment and your expectation as you go. Don't be driven by obligation. Be driven by passion and freedom.

A life driven by obligation will wear you down. Our approach to life should be driven by an understanding of what we are trying to accomplish, and why it's important to us. Then we will be free from obligation and instead driven by choice. You will no longer say, "I have to go to work." Instead you will consider the real benefits of your work in relation to your core desires. You might find that your work allows you to contribute to the world, to bring food to your family, to get out of the house, to meet people, and even to enjoy an occasional luxury! If you can't say that about your job, then find another. If you benefit from your job, then cherish it.

Your journey never ends. You never reach a point in your life where you stop improving. Don't have the concept that you will put in your time until you can finally get ahead of the game and put your feet up. It never happens that way. Consider the case of a famous musician who has "made it." Do you think he will sit back and relax, now that he's a big name? He is more likely to work even harder, only because of his fame, he will have even more demands on his time. And of course, new opportunities will emerge. Greater accomplishments open unforeseen possibilities on many levels, and there is no limit to your creativity, potential, or to your desire to be more today than you were yesterday.

The great prize at the end of the road is a great illusion; there is no ultimate prize at the end of some dark tunnel. The prize is the journey itself, and you can choose to make it a glorious one. Define for yourself what kind of effort you want to put into something, be mindful of your ownership of your journey, and you will find inspiration and satisfaction as you go. If you feel that your road is somehow wrong for you, then stop and take another look at your choices. If your goals are challenging, then your path won't be easy, but that is not to say it won't be exciting. Life should be captivating and interesting, so choose well and keep a clear and uplifted perspective. Then you will know the joy of the living.

Take time every week to consider how much you are willing to invest in your goals. The universe grants treasures to those who are willing to work. When you choose to recognize what's important to you and confirm that importance through your actions, without complaining and without backing down on your commitment, unexpected opportunities emerge over time. Also, when it's your choice, the journey becomes exciting in and of itself.

3) What am I Willing to Renounce?

Purity has always held a fascination for me. An untouched stretch of coastline, pristine water flowing and crashing down a mountainside, a clear mind, a healthy body and a soul free from pollution. The essence of something is always perfect, but as soon as we allow pollution to taint it, it becomes repulsive. A tiny amount of pollution introduces a foul quality even to the most majestic masterpiece of nature, and the humblest blade of grass is magnificent within a pure environment. Because of this fact, we cannot set our sights on perfection without thinking about stripping away imperfections. That's why I describe the discovery of a constraint like unearthing hidden treasure. I don't mean that the constraint itself is a treasure, but we need to see into the dark places in our souls if we are ever going to be free. You can't purify yourself if you don't discover your wounds and faults.

When we look deep within, we will discover some dreadful places. But we will also become familiar with the great gifts latent within us. These innate gifts are brought to light as we practice self-awareness. As we strip away our impurities and the restrictions created by our lower nature, we will unleash stunning inner beauty and strength. When Michelangelo beheld a nine-ton marble block, he saw a treasure completely invisible to any other man. "I saw the angel in the marble, and carved until I set him free," he said about the *David* statue. When he stripped away the excess, the world could see the majesty latent in the stone.

Life is about finding your core, and then stripping away everything that does not match your pure and perfect essence, so that what you have seen all along will become visible and manifest to the world. In order to honor our calling, we must create room for possibilities to unfold. When we renounce negative or empty elements, we create space, and we become free to invite something glorious to take its place.

Occasionally, look at your list and ask yourself, "What is it about me, or about my life, that doesn't match the future I envision?" Then get to work on carving away these things. I am fully aware of the difficulty that this task entails, but it is an essential task. We can't expect to develop new habits if we are not prepared to let go of old ones. We cannot expect new realities to unfold, new belief patterns, new levels of success or new adventures to become part of our lives if we cling to undesirable old patterns. The more we are prepared to renounce our baggage, the more room is left for transformation, and for a higher calling to manifest.

When I was young, I used to have a common diagnosis called ADHD, or Attention Deficit Hyperactivity Disorder, and I took daily medication for seven years. I realized one day however that this medication was destructive to me. I learned that it stimulates the central nervous system, that it was lowering my brain function and inhibiting my creativity and intelligence. Also, the medication does nothing to cure, but merely covers up symptoms. A powerful force outside myself compelled me to stop.

After seven years of taking this medication, every part of me except that force was against stopping, but I decided to do it anyway. The first five days were a nightmare. I could not focus on anything. I couldn't get any work done, I couldn't play music, and when I tried to play basketball, I couldn't make a single basket. Every night I was quivering, and I realized that I had been addicted to a powerful pharmaceutical drug. However, on the sixth day, something happened that transformed my inner consciousness, and after three weeks my body had completely changed (more details about this in Chapter 7). As I learned to master my body, now free from medication, my neurons began to function more precisely. I was more creative, had more energy, and was happier than ever before.

Another experience I had with transformation through self-denial came through my decision to abstain from sex. I had embraced sexuality as an integral part of life and didn't see why I should practice restraint if a beautiful woman crossed my path. But I came to some realizations, and then one day, I decided it was time for change. I decided never again to have sex outside of a long-term committed relationship, and that I would never again practice self-stimulation. Having such tremendous sexual energy in my body was stressful and painful, but after about three weeks it became a lot easier. I began to master it, and was able to channel my sexual energy into creativity, writing, playing music, doing sports, etc. I experienced great energy and freedom, and I was able to invest in truly meaningful things. I followed my conscience and my best interests in deciding to remain abstinent, and I am grateful for the peace and strength I gained as a result.

Another reason for my decision, was that I was preparing to eventually devote myself to the unfound love of my life. It was precious to me, this tender duty of becoming ready to take one woman to be my eternal partner. I surrendered the need to chase after girls, something that had always held my utmost fascination. I discovered that I can appreciate a flower without having to pluck it from its roots. I realized that it is by nurturing a flower and seeing it grow and blossom that we uncover the deepest treasures of human life.

A third and final example of doing away with a negative influence in my life was the most difficult for me. I decided to separate from two of my dearest friends. Many years ago, I was under the guidance of a mentor. When I first met him, I was so impressed that I paid almost ten thousand dollars to participate in his leadership training program. As time progressed, we developed a close friendship. At that time, I also had a beautiful girlfriend whom I treasured deeply. I cared deeply about them both, as I still do, but one day I was startled by a realization. I had become dependent on them, and I was always seeking their validation. Suddenly I could see clearly that these two relationships were damaging to me, but also to my two friends. Again, my heart compelled me to make a change.

I wrote them a letter explaining my thoughts and my heart. I praised them for all they had given me and prayed that they would understand and be granted something better. This experience tore me apart. I didn't sleep for days, and I spent several days in deep sorrow. Luckily, I had fantastic friends who were up with me all night, and who made hot cocoa with whipped cream to make me feel better. (You know who you are, and you know that I love you.) After a while I recovered. I became filled with renewed strength and clarity. I knew that I had made the right choice, and that my decision benefited my friends as much as it did me. And I knew that one day our paths would cross again.

In this same way I stopped drinking alcohol, I stopped watching TV, I stopped being so angry or worried or self-conscious. I overcame many other destructive habits. Not once have I regretted these decisions.

I tell you this because I know how terribly difficult it is to let go of something you care about, or something that has been right, or at least seemed right, for so long. But I also know how profoundly valuable it is to follow your heart. I am of course not suggesting that you should let go of the same things I did. Those things were obstacles for me at given times in my life, but your destination and your journey will not be the same as any other man's. You must figure out what you want and where you're going. Let your heart guide you. If you do, you will discover the path to your freedom and to the fulfillment of your potential.

No longer is it enough to post an affirmation on your bedroom door. It is no longer enough to learn another quick fix. You must pursue a higher value in life, and a higher value within yourself. Only from a sense of clarity can you achieve what you truly desire. The great discovery of your core desires, and of your calling, remains for you to make.

Traits of a Leader

Chapter 3

«Do not follow where the path may lead. Go instead where there is no path and leave a trail.»

~Ralph Waldo Emerson

As I traveled around the world, I realized that the most serious global shortage is not of food, resources, or shelter, but rather a far-reaching absence of true leadership. We seem to have abandoned the rites of passage, educational structures, and family and religious traditions that used to make men of us. From birth through school and in our jobs, we learn to follow. Instead of being inspired to making meaningful changes to the world, or even to our own lives, we are encouraged to flow with the current. An independent, non-conformant, intelligent thought is treated as unnecessary and even out of place. As a result, many men of this generation are unable to take responsibility for themselves, let alone for a relationship with a woman and the leadership of a family.

In her heart, every woman desires to be swooned by a man's strong and tender lead. Through his provision, she gains confidence and strength to bear and raise children. Through his fidelity and attention, she experiences herself as worthy and beautiful. Modern gender roles are confused, and the basics of feminine and masculine interaction are gradually fading. Without the polarity of masculine and feminine roles, natural attraction disappears. It's for us to stand up and mature into men who can lead well. If we do, we'll meet a great need in many lives, but especially in that of our beloved.

It may be comfortable to remain as a sheep among sheep or to work for position within the system as a kind of shepherd. The leadership I am here to encourage, though, is not about overseeing sheep. It's about challenges and risks, about pursuing meaningful success, and about developing rich relationships and personal maturity. A true leader doesn't need people to obey his directives just so he can feel powerful. The greatest leader is above all else the greatest servant. He takes responsibility for challenges, accepts blame if something goes wrong, shares praise when he's successful, draws out the leader in those around him, and dedicates himself to the well-being of others.

It's quite possible to survive for months without having a single intelligent thought cross our minds. We have the wisdom of the ages at our fingertips these days, but we're so much more likely to use our devices to zone out rather than to rise. To become free to think for ourselves requires great courage and the willingness to trust our own principles. In this chapter we will investigate five traits which are fundamental to leadership: curiosity, contemplation, purpose, empathy and responsibility. We will use this framework to shape the mind of a true leader.

Curiosity

"There is one thing I learned that changed everything. I immediately became successful and all the mysteries of the universe unfolded before me. "What? What was that thing?? Exactly."

Early in life, we come to see the world in a certain way. We go about our routines and tend to dismiss other views and ways as false, without any real question ever entering our minds. In this way we develop the spiritual blindness of the men in the elephant metaphor of Chapter One. For a true leader this is not enough. For us to realize success, to cultivate personal appeal, and to make sense of this world, it is not enough.

A true leader can't follow blindly a single religion or philosophy; he is compelled to study all of them. Likewise, he can't feel content with studying only one view of economics, politics, psychology, science, relationship theory, etc. He can't help but explore them all, and he's free to integrate these ideas with his own. His mind is alive with a broad and vibrant worldview that expands each day.

Questions generate growth. Whatever great abilities you have today, you developed because your curiosity sustained over time. If you are good at basketball today, it is because you were curious about it sometime in the past. You asked questions such as "What does it mean to be a good basketball player?" "Why do I want to become good?" and finally, "How can I become better?" You kept asking these questions, and eventually you became a good player. At one point you might have said, "This is how to play basketball." That was the point at which you stopped improving.

It is the questions that we need, because no single solution holds the key to self-realization. It's curiosity itself that we must cultivate. Very often when someone asks me a good question, my answer to them is, "Exactly." For instance, if they ask, "How can I attract the woman of my dreams?" my answer will be, "Exactly." The many answers to their question will come to them over time if they remain curious. The questions are what matters, and the need to know is what brings success. If I were to give them a definitive answer, I might be guilty of making them feel satisfied.

Wisdom accommodates life's many variables, such as where you are in life, your social setting, and your companions. We can't expect one answer to fit all circumstances. When we are constantly looking for a quick fix or an instant answer, we are giving away the treasure that a question alone provides, closing our minds and killing our curiosity. A "correct" answer may give us a small shot of relief, a little sphere of comfort, but it will never make us grow. To grow we must open our minds, expand our spirits and explore the unknown.

Curiosity is not only a vital component to grow as a person, it's equally important in connecting with people. By cultivating curiosity, we can make people open their hearts to us. We must, of course, be people worthy of trust, but of equal importance, we must be truly, candidly, genuinely interested in people.

When talking to a woman, be curious about everything that hides behind her lovely facade. Wonder what her insecurities are, what her passions are, what moves her, what makes her feel alive and what makes her smile. Let these, along with a million other questions buzz around your mind as you talk with her, regardless of how long you have known her. Because of your curiosity she will become curious, and you immediately separate yourselves from the world in an exciting and vibrant bubble. In this bubble your minds expand, and you become something greater than yourselves in the presence of one another. You feel liberated and expressive, alive and impregnated with anticipation and emotion. Fascinating and colorful experiences occur in moments like these, and it all starts with curiosity.

Curiosity is an essential part of life. It's a driving force that energizes you and engages other people. Casanova used to say that "Love is three-quarters curiosity," and like love, it can't be forged, because it's more a state of mind than a practiced technique. You cannot, for instance, memorize questions to ask a girl, because then they are no longer true questions. They are the prepackaged answer to the question, "What should I ask a woman?" The only real answer is that there is no one question to ask. Instead you must be curious about her. You must cultivate curiosity, invite it into your life, embrace the feeling of not knowing, and refuse to settle for any one answer.

An artist approaches a clean canvas with a fresh mind. Approach a new relationship as you would a fresh canvas, with the confidence to offer a woman your colors and the ability to appreciate the value of hers. She will sense your strength and that you have something to offer her. She will cherish the power of perception that allows you to truly see her and know that you have the capacity to taste the depth of her beauty. With this vision in mind, with pure color and light clearly in your heart, and sharing a white canvas, you can invite her to paint with you. In a moment apart, free from disturbances and hidden agendas, brilliant encounters arise.

Continue this practice as your relationship matures. Don't let familiarity fill your life with boredom. Always remain curious and the depth of your intimacy will have no end. As humans we are experts at finding answers. Whenever we ask ourselves a question, we come up with an answer, and are confident that we are correct. We are satisfied, like the boy who completed his 3rd grade unit on our planets and was confused upon meeting a great astronomer who was still stuck on that chapter. Our preoccupation should not be primarily with finding answers, but with finding the right questions.

The size of our life is in many ways determined by the size of our questions. Little minds ask small questions; great minds ask great questions. To become a greater man, you must elevate your questions.

"How can I approach this girl?" is a small question.

"How can I become a man who deserves her?" is better.

"How can I become a man who deserves the praise of my higher conscience, or of the people I meet each day, or even of the people of this wide world?" is even better.

We access our higher nature when we ask higher questions. They motivate us, keep us on the edge and keep us in touch with our purpose. We must never lose touch with our curiosity, never distance ourselves from the question, but instead, dance with it and become one with it. The answers may vary from time to time, but the questions themselves are eternal. Never let an answer restrain you; always seek mystery.

"So, what is the right question to ask?"

"Exactly."

Contemplation

When you take time to pause, you allow your mind to reset. You clear away distractions and allow yourself to see the things previously hidden. It is in these moments that new ideas, new inspirations, and new strengths come to you. Without the ability to pause and reflect, we risk becoming narrow-minded and unfocused. Without taking time to outline our course of action, we risk going in circles.

A common response to difficulty is to redouble our efforts. A wiser course of action is to slow down and discover a better path. Sometimes in our race to overcome challenges we fail to recognize that we are moving in the wrong direction, and we end up further and further away from our goal. We keep moving forward blindly, tunneling our way into a rabbit hole. The further in we go, the harder it is to see. We forget that we're in a hole and lose sight of any and all options. We end up doing what we have always done, digging deeper down. We repeat our failed strategies, expecting new results. "Madness," as Einstein would say.

When we notice that increased efforts don't lead us closer to our goal, we suffer the fear of running out of power. It is like running on a treadmill, speeding up when we recognize we aren't going anywhere. Our path through life should be marked by simplicity and delight, our decisions should be made based on clarity, and our efforts should be mindful. If we want to escape the rabbit hole, it doesn't help to dig further. First, we need a little time to pause and reflect.

When I was young, our family used to treasure the quiet times we shared as a family. My dad loved our boat; he would go out to our favorite little island, set anchor, head for shore with his favorite camping chair and enjoy his precious Tuborg beer. This was the moment he felt peace in his life, perhaps the most important moments in his life. Every summer we created these fond memories, but I also remember the toxic efforts to get ready.

My dad worked hard all year to save for a bigger boat and better equipment. He came home stressed and exhausted, unable to enjoy the simple delights of everyday life. The weeks before our trip, our house was turned upside down with preparations. Mom would run around making sure everything was in order. On the day itself my sister and I had better not do anything fun, because our mom would constantly shout our names to make sure we were ready. No one could find a peaceful corner. We rushed off to the shore, hurried to ready the boat, and raced to the island. Forget about the stunning fjords and breathtaking panorama unfolding before us moment by moment. Finally, when we reached the Island and the boat was secured, my dad could bring out his precious camping chair, pop open his cold one, and take a deep relaxing breath.

My Viking heritage had helped him fight his way through blood and money for his annual portion of peace. In many ways this moment was what my dad lived for. He worked his whole life to achieve this fleeting feeling of peace and quietude. As I look back, I realize that if he were to have walked over to our refrigerator one day, taken out an ice cold Tuborg, walked out into our lovely garden, and taken a deep soothing breath, he may have accomplished the same coveted peace.

In this era of TV, radio, cell phones and the internet governing our lives, we are provided with a steady stream of miscellaneous stimulation. When we are thus distracted, we fail to recognize that the beauty we search for is right in front of us. As this constant barrage of sounds, images and data works its way into our subconscious, we lose the sense of our core. We lose our ability to make decisions because this pop culture buzz informs our decisions and makes up our minds for us. When we are never focused or clear to make our own decisions, we become a product of the whims of others, shedding our unique qualities. Ultimately, we forget the things that are truly important to us. Our lives become a shadow of what we desire, what we intend. Our satisfaction comes then only from the distractions. We fail to see the greater beauty, and we keep fighting for an elusive sense of joy that never seems to come to us.

When we redirect our attention towards the higher values in life, we are once again free to see the true beauty hidden in this world. Every day we do this through our morning ritual, and we must extend this practice throughout the day. Whenever you get tempted to indulge in your lower nature, or when you feel lazy or stressed, take a moment to pause. Then take up your list and redirect your attention to your higher nature. Allow this to fill you with strength, courage, motivation and joy.

Take time to reset your mind. Invest in what makes you relax: take a walk in the garden with a nice beverage, go fishing, meditate, take a hot bath, go for a run, or shoot some hoops. Do this by yourself free from distraction. Do not worry about your problems at this time, they will still be there when you return.

When you hike up a mountain, you must occasionally take of your backpack, enjoy the scenery for a moment, and regain your strength. No one will steal your baggage, no one wants it. It will still be there when you return, only through your pause, you will have regained the strength and clarity to carry it.

Our baggage tends to wear us down, and we forget about the beauty all around us. So, when you take off your backpack, remember the things you love, and offer thanks. There are always things to be grateful for, so use this moment to remember them. As the Buddhist proverb states,

"Maybe you didn't learn so much today, at least you learned something, and if you didn't learn anything, at least you didn't get sick, and if you got sick, at least you didn't die, so let us be grateful."

Ultimately a peaceful mind filled with appreciation is the greatest resource we can have. We must therefore grant ourselves this ritual of taking time to pause and reflect. It is in these moments we find greatness. The solution to our problems is often far closer than we first believe. Sometimes it's as close as the Tuborg, the garden, and that all-important deep breath. Truthfully, happiness is right around the corner; greatness is right across the street. All we need to do is open our minds. The solution is not inside a rabbit hole and generally not waiting at the end of some torturous experiment born of wrong-headed desperation. It's a matter of discovering the right path by exploring options and thinking things through. So, remember to pause and reflect.

Purpose

After you have returned to a bright and appreciative state of mind, you are free once more to direct your attention to your purpose. In your purpose, you find your inner strength, and it provides the drive and vigor necessary to mature into an effective leader. Because of this added dimension of meaning, you exude the presence that inspires others to have confidence in you and to be drawn to you, intrigued by your passionate experience of life.

The Apocryphal Mark Twain says that "The two most important days of your life are the day you were born, and the day you find out why." Having meaning in your life fills you with the strength to overcome your personal challenges. Your constraints and doubts become less important, because you no longer have time to dwell on them. Viktor Frankl explains in his book, *Man's Search for Meaning*, that " Those who have a 'why' to live, can bear with almost any 'how.'" When you discover your "why", you start to tap into hidden resources that drive you to excellence.

The more defined and vivid your purpose is, the more glorious your life will be, but it requires that your purpose is rooted in your core reasoning. Certainly, it's possible to accomplish grand superficial things in life without clear core reasoning, but such accomplishments will never lead to complete fulfillment. If your life's goal is to become rich and famous, to impress women, or receive recognition from your peers you will at some point run out of energy. This purpose is not good enough to motivate you in the long run. When your actions are governed by a narrow vision, you will be blind to the greater meaning in life.

The greatest fulfillment is found in the service of others. Jesus Christ said that those who seek to lose their lives will gain it. Think therefore about what you can do to contribute to the world. Think not only of your own, but of the happiness of others. There is nothing wrong with pursuing money and recognition in order to serve a higher purpose, but we must never lose focus of the quintessence. When we set our minds on a higher purpose, the cosmic intelligence will provide us with all the resources we need; inspiration, strength and courage will inevitably come to us.

A planet that spins around its own axis disconnected from a larger galactic network will eventually wither. A planet must revolve around its own axis, but also move in harmony with the rest of the solar system. Only when we link our purpose to a higher ideal, can we access the hidden resources that sustain our journey.

A high value woman doesn't want to be her man's only focus. Imagine if one day you were sent out to defend your country in war. How would your woman respond? She would fall into despair, embrace you in anguish, and beg you to stay with her. She would want you to know how much she needs you, how much she loves and cares for you, and how crushed she would be if anything happened to you. Through this tender emotion she strengthens you and stirs in you the longing to overcome and to return to her loving embrace. But deep inside she knows you must leave. You yourself might be terrified, but you know what you must do.

Imagine if you just said, "Yeah you're right, screw our country, I'd much rather stay here with you!" She might be relieved for a while, maybe even a couple of weeks, but eventually her heart will feel empty. She will sense that she's draining your courage, and that she's compromising your masculinity, strength and purpose. If you're not a better man because of the love you share, if she cannot inspire greatness in you, then she can't escape the feeling of guilt.

To discover meaning to our existence we must ask ourselves, "why." Look at your list in the morning and ask yourself why these things are important to you, and what they will ultimately give you. How does your choices contribute to the people around you? Does your list reflect a purpose you're willing to live and die for? Let this dialogue play in the back of your mind throughout the day. Ask yourself why you go to work, why you're reading this book, why you exercise. Find the motivation behind your actions, and you will tap into inspiration and strength. Do this also when you are indulging your lower nature. When you eat fast food, or treat people poorly, or watch a sitcom, find the courage to challenge yourself. Ask, "Why am I doing this?" And if there is no glory in your answer, then change your course.

Empathy

True empathy is obtained when you experience other people's emotions as your own, when their suffering becomes your suffering, and when their joy becomes your joy. In our individualistic society we cry out for freedom, forgetting that individual freedom is impossible without collective freedom. You may exercise your freedom to play drums at the middle of the night, but this robs your neighbor from his freedom to sleep. Empathy is a powerful force that drives us to make the world a better place. When we share each other's joys and burdens, we can move beyond the injustice and violence, lawsuits and wars that have marred our history. True leadership, and true freedom, can only be obtained through empathy.

We have all heard that we must obey the Golden Rule and "do onto others as we would have them do unto us", but this is not enough. We must realize that we all have unique needs and longings and learn to see life through the eyes of others. We can obtain this spiritual ability by learning to value the needs of others before our own, and by learning to observe their gestures and facial expressions. When you interact with someone, ask yourself the question, "How can I best serve this person?" And then do your best to offer your service. Remember, the greatest leader is the greatest servant.

Of course, not everyone shares the view that life is enhanced by selfless love. You are sure to run into people who dislike your views or your efforts to reach out to them. It's hard to care for people who don't reciprocate, but it is a worthy and necessary discipline. After all, what profits us if we can only reach those who are kind to us? We must learn not to judge, but instead understand and accept people as they are, recognize what shaped them, and imagine what life looks like in their shoes. The more difficult the relationship, the greater our opportunity will be to mature through the challenge. The fruit of this maturity of heart is the ability to lead anyone authentically and effectively.

Sacrificial love opens the path to the greatest inner fulfillment and often to social and financial success as well. Suppose you have ten friends. Imagine that one morning, you demand that each one give you all their money. Of course, it's likely that by noon you will have lost ten friendships. Imagine that instead you take each of them aside and make them feel free to share their thoughts with you. What if you were able to solve some vexing personal problem for each of the ten. It wouldn't be long before each friend had brought another ten to meet you, and soon enough, you would be well known in your community.

I'm not suggesting that you let people take advantage of you, or that you should please people just to avoid conflict. It's easy to look the other way when someone does something you believe to be wrong, but that's indifference and taking the easy way out. We must have the courage and resolve to look out for the best interests of others. Sometimes people need kindness, sometimes a frank or harsh word, and sometimes even silence. Develop your intuition and allow your heart to guide you. You will find that you'll know the right thing to do.

Personally, I can't stand it when someone I care about acts foolishly, and fail to live up to their full potential, so I tell them exactly so. However, I do my best to consider what the person needs to hear, rather than what I want to tell them. I try to renounce my self-interest and not worry about appearing like the bad guy, because I know that eventually they will realize the love behind my words. Merely being polite is often a weakness and a betrayal, a low form of self-interest. Empathy calls us beyond self-interest, beyond our comfort zone, beyond the cool pleasantries of the merely polite, and into the greater love, effort and insight of true leadership.

Responsibility

Lord of the Rings is my favorite movie trilogy. I love it because of its cinematic brilliance and intriguing plot, but more importantly, because it offers invaluable insights into the human condition. Each of the main characters comes to a moment of decision which affects the destiny of their world, Middle Earth, and they each save the day in their own way. Aragorn gives up the shadowed path of a ranger, accepts the sword of Elendil, and returns to the Kingship of Gondor. Theoden sends soldiers to defend someone else's kingdom. Faramir allows Frodo to keep the Ring, knowing that the law requires him to bring it to his homeland and that the penalty for failing to do so is death. The one who bears the greatest burden speaks for all of them and us as well when he tells Gandalf that he wishes that none of this had come to him. Gandalf counsels Frodo that "so do all who live to see such times. But that is not for them to decide. All we have to decide is what to do with the time that is given us."

During my travels in the Dominican Republic I came upon the scene of a terrible accident. I was riding on the back of a motorcycle on my way home from my scuba diving class when I saw a big gathering of people. As we drove further, we saw a motorcycle lying on the side of the road. A few hundred feet further a man was lying on the ground. He was in excruciating pain. His leg was completely ripped off, his muscles were twisted, and he had lacerations all the way to the bone all over his body. We pulled over to help. I asked the collection of about thirty people if they had called the ambulance, and they answered, "Yes". Since I was the only one in the crowd who spoke English and the injured was British, I had to be the one to comfort him. I told him to look me straight in the eyes and not focus on anything else, knowing if he saw his body he might go into shock. I was amazed that he was still conscious.

As minutes passed and he lost more blood, I asked again if anyone had called the ambulance. They answered, "Yes", but this time I demanded to see the actual person who called. It turned out that no one had called the ambulance! A few minutes later an ambulance did in fact come by, but to my great shock it slowly passed us without stopping. No one was ready to take responsibility to save this man's life, not even the ambulance driver. Everyone assumed that someone else would do it. I finally realized that it was up to me to call the ambulance. A few minutes later it showed up, and we all had to leave. The police were surely on their way, and if we had been found at the scene, we would have been held in jail for the night for questioning.

I realized that day that the question of who is at fault is completely irrelevant. What matters is who chooses to take responsibility. Many people are suffering in this world, and the fact is, you and I can do something about it. If you have a unique ability, or if you see a need, then do what you can to be the agent of change.

If you see someone who struggles to perform a task, instead of telling yourself, "It's not my job, it's not my problem," either offer your help with humility, or fix the problem without the person knowing. Do this, not because it will bring you a reward, but because it is the best possible thing to do. Make the commitment that as a leader, you will always strive for excellence. Do not consider your relationships as fifty-fifty contracts, both partners must give one hundred percent for it to work. If you make it a habit to offer your assistance wherever you are needed, then you will develop a strong and generous nature that enables you to weather the challenges that every relationship faces.

It is true that most problems, even many of your personal problems, are not your fault. We are shaped greatly by our environment and other factors beyond our control. The state of the world around you is not your fault either; you'll be happy to know that you are not to blame for all the war, despair and evil in the world. In one sense, though, it just doesn't matter that we aren't directly responsible for this or that problem. The question of who is to blame is irrelevant. In fact, the ones to blame are usually not the ones who end up taking responsibility. What matters is who decides to make a difference. Once you decide to act for what you think is right, people will see strength in you, trust you, and look to you for guidance.

People in general, and women in particular, are drawn to a man who demonstrates character. As you become a leader and a man of integrity, your woman will feel the freedom to surrender herself to the security of your embrace, safe in the knowledge that the love you share will endure. When a woman feels protected by a man of character, she cares little whether he is well built physically, has strong muscles or a deep voice. She can freely surrender to him, knowing that he will be there for her, to protect her from any threat, and to satisfy the deep yearnings in her heart.

Pathway to Women

Section 2

Women are at once mystical and magical. **Section II** *seeks to uncover the heart and mind of a woman and lays out the strategies and mindsets required to succeed in a relationship.*

A Woman's Yearnings
Chapter 4

«By all means, marry. If you get a good wife, you'll become happy; if you get a bad one, you'll become a philosopher.»

~Socrates

The greatest mystery for men throughout history has been to understand the mind and heart of a woman. An unknown author once wrote that understanding what a woman wants is like trying to figure out the fragrance of the color seven. Internationally acclaimed physicist and cosmologist Stephen Hawking once stated that the greatest puzzle in the universe is not a scientific or mathematical problem, but the enigma presented by womankind. This confusion about women stems from our persistent expectation that they should behave like men. The fact that they are entirely different creatures, with different priorities, brain patterns and needs, entirely escapes us.

In order to unravel the ancient mystery presented by a woman, we must first acknowledge that despite the standards society has pushed upon her, she is still at heart a woman, with her unique yearnings, desires and needs. This chapter delves into the unique qualities of women and seeks to uncover their fundamental needs and yearnings.

Yearnings & Longings

Women have always fascinated me. In kindergarten when other boys were mean to the girls and scared of their "cooties", I would ponder them in awestruck fascination. My fascination has grown ever since. I am utterly amazed by the beauty, softness and mystery of women. Later I made the happy discovery that a true lover of women is loved by them in return.

Men might be satisfied with throwing on their oil-stained t-shirt from three days back in the morning, but a woman will take her sweet time to make sure she looks flawless. She will pay special attention to ensure her attire is matching, are reflective of her mood, and highlights her natural charm and beauty. Does she do this to marvel at her magnificence every time she passes a mirror? Of course not. She wants to be adored for her unique feminine attributes. The first step to winning a woman's heart is simple: notice her.

Men are generally excellent at showering their girl with affection as they first meet. They gaze at her brilliant curves, complement her on her cute dress, send her adoring texts, open the door for her, take her to expensive restaurants and buy her exquisite jewelries to complement her incomparable beauty. They go to immeasurable lengths to express their undying love, and so their girl basks in their adoration. As time passes, and they believe they have won her unwavering faithfulness, their displays of affection gradually start to fade. In tandem with their negligence, the fire in their relationship slowly disappears.

Let me draw you a picture to illustrate what quenches the fire in a relationship over time. Let's say you wake up in the morning and everything is fine. You go to work without any drama. Your sweetheart sees you out and you kiss her goodbye. Her eyes glow with an unspoken message: "I can't wait till he gets back home. Oh, how I adore him." As soon as you leave, she runs to the store with you on her mind to purchase the best commodities to prepare your favorite meal. She then goes to color her hair, to put on a sexy dress, to clean and decorate your home. She then goes to help your mom in the elderly home. All that with you on her mind. She's so excited about the thought of you coming home, about the intimacy you will share, and about all the stories she will tell you. Her nurturing side is making her heart pound with a sweet yearning for your return.

Now let me show you how things go south:

You come home tired after a long day. You hardly notice her nor what she's wearing nor the decorations. She comes to sit near you, to ask you about your day and to share her stories with you, but instead of listening, you turn on your favorite TV show. Her continence shuts down. "Why would I put in effort and attention when he doesn't even notice?" She shrinks at the thought that you lost your attraction for her. She wonders if another girl has captured your attention. Then she stops herself and says: "He must be having an awful day. I'll make sure to shower him with affection tomorrow as well, then everything will be wonderful again." Then tomorrow comes, and the same thing happens. So does the next day, and the next day. This pattern repeats itself until eventually her eager yearning hopelessly transforms into a desperate longing.

Because of our inexhaustible ignorance and unavoidable tendency of screwing up, we men are bound to get on a woman's nerve from time to time. But genuine adoration from a place of sincerity without hidden motives, will get us a long way in recovering her affection. A woman yearning for our love, our touch and our affection, is the ultimate destination for a man in a relationship. She will shower us with endless treasures and make our lives a fairytale of wonderment. But when we neglect her, and her yearning turns into longing, our relationships that were once filled with joy and excitement, will turn into our worst nightmare.

What separates yearnings and longings? Yearning is a passionate desire for something close to our reach. It's this anticipation for your touch, your affection, and your love, that makes a woman bubble with excitement. This yearning is what we must stimulate and nurture. Longing, on the other hand, involves the same deep desire but stripped from the hope in its fulfillment. Chasing a dream just outside our reach is what makes life exhilarating, but when we remove the hope, all desire turns into desperation. It makes a woman feel powerless, helpless, or even enraged. When her needs go unmet for too long, and her yearnings turn into longings, she loses the taste for life, and her desperation gives rise to complaints and irrational behaviors.

When men lament in bewilderment over a woman's irrational behaviors, her sudden outbursts, her constant complaints over seemingly insignificant things, it's because they fail to acknowledge the underlying cause. Men's confusion about women stems from nothing else than their failure to provide her basic needs and yearnings.

Women are not complicated, but they have an unquenchable need to be seen for who they truly are. Just like a man, a woman has a higher and a lower self. Her lower self is filled with fear, frustration, desperation and pain. Her higher self is her divine identity that links her to the cosmic intelligence and represents the quintessence of her beauty. A woman yearns for a man who can see the divinity within her and bring it to surface. A man capable of this will provide her with the sweetest gifts and the path to her supreme fulfillment. A man who can't, will make her longing for an elusive unobtainable dream. He will then join the endless multitudes of men bewildered by women's irrational behaviors.

Practice appreciating your woman. It is undoubtably a skill and a discipline. Over time you will discover hidden beauty within her. If you've seen the movie *Men in Black*, then you remember the scene when the viewer realizes that the missing galaxy is inside the charm on the cat's collar. Only the practiced eye of a curious and sensitive lover will be able to see the infinity of beauty in his lady. This transcendent beauty is timeless and priceless, and the more you engage it, the more it transforms your relationship.

In Chapter 11, we will discover how to express our affection for our girl, but it all starts with our abilities to see divinity within her. If you gaze at your sweetheart with eyes of adoration, your energy will heal and remake her. This is not only true because you see her with generous and tender eyes, but because your love transforms her. The joy you feel when you're with her is like sunshine for her garden, and she will reflect to you the adoration that you shower upon her.

A Woman is a Multiplier

An alteration of William Golding's quote says: "Whatever you give a woman, she will make greater. If you give her sperm, she'll give you a baby. If you give her a house, she'll give you a home. If you give her groceries, she'll give you a meal. If you give her a smile, she'll give you her heart. She multiplies and enlarges what is given to her. So, if you give her crap, she will give you tons of shit." When your girl is behaving toxic, remember to ask yourself: "What have I given her lately?"

If you see a woman that is sluggish, messy, unorganized, untimely, depressed, irresponsible and unkempt, look at her spouse and ask how well he cares for her, pays attention to her, kisses her, and provides for her. Often you will see that her uninspired behavior is a direct reflection of her spouse's inability to meet her yearnings.

A woman is not perfect, she will struggle with many of the same challenges you struggle with. However, in many ways, her state of mind is a reflection of the types of nourishments you provide for her. If you provide her with uplifting words, affectionate gestures, assuring acts and a gentle touch, she will convert these elements into wonderful expressions of love and beauty. It is these perpetual exchanges that give life to the heart of a relationship.

Playfulness

Don't allow your life to be drowned by endless routines. Spark your love-life with excitement whenever you can. Many relationships resemble social contracts more than love affairs. It leads me to wonder what happens to the butterflies, to the passion and lifeforce that courses through their veins when couples first meet? People say they need time for their careers and responsibilities, and don't have time to enjoy life anymore. The natural consequence of this decision is of course that the fire in their love-life eventually wanes. When your relationship is dry, free from excitement and fun, it will leave you exhausted, and your attraction withers from boredom.

Spark your relationship by creating fond memories. Take her on an exciting vacation to a new and exotic destination. Invite her on an date out of the ordinary. Take her mountain-climbing, dolphin swimming, camelback riding, bobsledding, or cage diving with sharks. Infuse your life with excitement that's out of the ordinary. More important than these seasonal outings, however, is that you develop a personality that's fun and spontaneous.

Personally, I never miss a chance to be playful. Once when I was sharing a hostel with some friends in the Caribbean, I got up early to buy water guns. I filled them, tossed some by my sleeping friends, squirted them awake and ran for cover! I used to blow soap bubbles in arbitrary venues. I'll never forget how people's expressions of bewilderment slowly transformed into laughter and delight. When traveling through the blue lagoon, Jamaica, my friends and I decided to sneak into Tom Cruise's estate. We parked our canoes by the private beach, convinced the guard that we were renting the villa nearby, and climbed the fence into the estate. It was only when the dogs came storming, we realized we had to run for our lives!

It's well worth it to lighten up, and to explore the endless adventures life has to offer. Take her on an occasional intriguing date, or on a minimoon (a miniature honeymoon), but more importantly, learn to charm your girl, and enjoy your everyday life with her. It's okay to mess up sometimes and do something silly. It's charming to laugh at yourself, and even to laugh at her. It will ultimately spark excitement into your love-life.

Mischief

When I was little, I made the marvelous discovery that it's easy to win someone's affection by making them pretend to be offended. Ever since that discovery, I have loved to do mischief. For instance, I used to steal apples from my neighbor's tree and then leave a note telling how delicious they tasted. The next time I saw them I would give them a big smile, and then run away. Those neighbors adored me. They pretended to be mad, but they adored me.

Still to this day, I never miss the chance to make fun of people. It's my greatest satisfaction. If I see my girl standing on her toes, struggling to reach the top shelf. I resist the urge to run to her assistance. Instead, I stand close by and watch her. She starts to feel self-conscious and embarrassed at how silly she looks. After I have teased her enough, I say in the most charming manner I can: "How may I be of assistance, my royal shortness?" I wink at her and offer my assistance like a proper gentleman.

Picture the little kid with his hand stuck in the cookie jar with a big guilty smile on his face. That was me. I got away with devouring those forbidden cookies because of the unquenchable power of charm. Another kid would have dropped the goods and begged for mercy. Of course, he might have gotten off the hook, but he wouldn't have kept the cookie. True charm is the little kid that looks up at his mother with a big innocent smile. His eyes say it all, "All right... hee hee, you got me! I've been extremely naughty...but you still love me! And there's no way I'm giving this cookie back!" His mother looks at him and pretends to be angry, yet she can't help but marvel at his charm and mischief.

There is a difference between malicious mischief, which hurts people, and the teasing that leads to a shared experience. And, of course, people have unique differences in what they perceive as funny or enjoyable. But every woman likes to know that her man enjoys life and especially that he enjoys her. If you use your charm to draw your sweetheart out, then it will strengthen your bond and enhance your intimacy.

Assurance

When a woman gives her hand to a man, she leaves behind all the comforts of her home and surrenders to his loving and protective arms. The safety and warm embrace she used to receive from her father, now becomes his responsibility. He must prove to her that she can safely rest in his arms, knowing he has got her, and that he will never let go.

Parents would pay millions in ransom in case their daughter got kidnapped, and gladly lay down their lives to protect her. A real man should be able to hold her with this same protective parental impulse. He should be able to love her more than her father, mother and siblings. This assurance is what allows a woman to embrace her true innocence and beauty, and to blossom in her feminine qualities.

Today's society has many opinions about a woman's role in a relationship. Women's movements shout for independence, saying, "We can do it all ourselves!" Of course, they can do things themselves. Women are perfectly capable of doing most things men can do. The relevant question is not whether they can do it, but what's ideal. Our society has confused the ideas of position and value.

Man and woman represent two invaluable pieces in an intricate body. The liver doesn't say to the heart: "I want to be the one to pump blood!" If it did, the entire body would stop functioning. This universe is a body with specific functions, rules and principles. If we can't uphold these principles, then we are laying the groundwork for our destruction. To say

58

that the heart is more valuable than the liver is ludicrous, because the body would stop operating without either one. The integrity of the body depends on each entity fulfilling its unique irreplaceable role.

A man's role in a relationship is to provide safety, comfort, protection, and financial stability to the home. If he can't do that, a woman may be forced to take on a masculine role that conflicts with her original nature. The result is that she becomes burdened or overtaxed, and the stress is like a layer of fog preventing her true feminine qualities from emerging. Consequently, polarity fades, and so does the attraction necessary to stimulate the relationship with her man. There's no harmony, only sameness. There's no spark, only an asbestos substance. As the fire quietly disappears, so does the relationship.

In the society we live in, we have become so fixated with blending the roles of men and women that it has become hard for young people to recognize the unique inherent qualities presented by each gender. We are bombarded by social and environmental influences telling us what to think and what to feel, and we forget what is so obvious and right in front of us. Men today are terrified of even looking at a woman for more than two seconds, in fear of getting sued for harassment. This fear for women gets imprinted into a young man's inner fibers. He might be afraid to be masculine, afraid to say the wrong thing, or afraid to touch his woman and display his passion for her. This has resulted in a serious detriment in our society.

Please understand that I'm not suggesting that we push women into restrictive, predetermined roles. I am the first person to rally for women's rights. However, in the noble pursuit of gender equality, we have missed a critical point: that equality and sameness are dreadfully different concepts. In the past, women were denied basic civil rights, such as the right to vote and attend college with men, so they cried out for equality. But the societal drive we see today, leading women to push for total independence from men has an entirely different root. The desire for "liberation" from men, is largely caused by our failings. We have been self-centered, unreliable, and unable or unwilling to provide for their needs. They had to make do, and soon discovered that they were better off on their own. When men are flimsy, unstable, and immature, women become fretful as they live their lives in uncertainty. A relationship based on this bitter foundation is bound to crumble.

It's time to raise the bar as men; to reclaim our masculinity, pride, charisma, boldness, strength and confidence. To prove to our lady our abilities to provide her with shelter, comfort and stability. To reassure her that we will never leave her, that we will walk with her through all of life's trials, and that she can safely rest in our strong arms. If we can claim our nobility and masculinity, our lady will once again be liberated to embrace her sweet femininity, and warmth and beauty will naturally blossom in our relationships.

Raising our standards depends on developing our virtues and getting our lives together. Does a woman want a wealthy man? Absolutely. A hardworking, rich and generous man is almost every woman's dream. However, it's not money, but rather the way he handles himself and his success that provides assurance. In her intuitive heart, a woman knows the hidden wisdoms of the ages, that a real man is the one who knows that detachment does not mean owning nothing, but simply that nothing owns him. This knowing that things were made to be used, and people were made to be loved, not the other way around, is the saving grace that can not only ensure a thriving relationship but could save humankind from major calamities.

The next step is to develop our virtues. Even if we can obtain all the security, safety, and financial stability in the world, it will be meaningless unless we have developed our inner qualities. Without a sacrificial heart, a woman will not be able to surrender to our embrace. A virtue, by definition, is the moral excellence of a person. It includes kindness, honesty, service, benevolence, charity, generosity, patience, empathy, courage, hope, etc. It comes from a commitment to doing the right thing no matter the personal cost, from a willingness to resist impulses, urges or desires, and from a determination to act according to noble values and principles.

We must make the important distinction between virtue and niceness. Someone can be nice on the outside while being absolutely vicious on the inside. Of course, this is a step above being vicious all around, but we need to establish virtue as a part of our identity, by developing moral principles and by dedicating ourselves to living accordingly. Some people believe they possess absolute goodness because they never say or do anything that offends people. They have personified the archetypical "Nice Guy". Of course, nobody likes a "Nice Guy", because hidden within his niceness there is usually a hint of cowardness. He flees from conflict and is unwilling to stand up for his principles and to battle against wickedness. No one can respect him because he lacks integrity and self-respect.

If your woman is rebellious or bad mannered, you must be able to straighten her and inspire her higher self. If you stimulate her dark side by letting her walk all over you, she will never love nor respect you. She needs a man who is certain in his principles and strong enough to inspire her goodness and higher self. This is what builds trust in a relationship.

Virtue and maturity are the qualities that allow a woman to find comfort in your protection and love. It is embedded into her DNA to worry about all kinds of things. She worries about the laundry, her friend's daughter's spelling bee, global warming, what she will wear for the banquet next month, the toothache suffered by her distant cousin's cat, what to make for dinner, and a million other things. In order to stay balanced, she needs a man to welcome her into his arms and reassure her that things will be OK. She also needs to know that if a crisis does erupt, that she can trust him to work with her to resolve any pending disasters.

When you encounter disasters of your own, learn to work them through before turning to her for comfort or advice. Of course, there are appropriate times for you to share your concerns with her. It's important to allow her to exercise her nurturing side by caring for you and helping you. However, as a general rule, don't burden your lady with your troubles and insecurities. Instead, develop the maturity and confidence to resolve difficulties and inner conflicts as they emerge, and then be there to help her with her burdens as well. Through this practice, you will establish the fortitude necessary to cope with life and to support your darling's needs as well. This gift will free her to embrace her inner child and bring beauty and warmth into your home. Your strength and virtue are the secrets to your sweetheart's peace and confidence.

Romance

Families are usually inclined to shower their daughter with all her major needs. Brothers, sisters, parents, uncles, cousins and so forth are fully capable of providing shelter, food, clothing, care, money, etc., and they will do anything in their powers to shower her with gifts. However, there is one need her family is unable to, and shouldn't, provide for her: the need for romance. This is a need that can be exclusively met by her man. A man should be able to take over all the needs provided to a girl by her family, but it is the need for romance that stands as the pivotal substance in their relationship.

When a girl dreams of leaving her family to sail into the sunset with her prince charming, it is the need for romance that drives her desires. She dreams to be swept of her feet by a man able to hold her tightly in his arms and take her on a breathtaking adventure. It sounds like a fantasy ascribed to the diaries of teenage girls, but this need for romance lies dormant in every woman's heart. Even if a man provides for all her major needs, if he can't seduce her, and satisfy her deep romantic needs, she will forever live with a deep feeling of emptiness.

Men's failure in romancing a lady comes from the same fundamental confusion about a woman's nature. We expect her to be stimulated the same way we are, even though stimulating a man requires no finesse whatsoever. All we need is a couple of beers and the sight of a shape that vaguely resembles the feminine form and we are ready to go! Thinking a woman will be stimulated the same way is a bulletproof recipe for disaster.

Men's path to arousal resembles a microwave oven. All you need to do is flip a switch and it gets hot in a matter of seconds. A woman is more like a slow roasting rotisserie. She needs time to warm up, to reach tenderness, and for her juices to simmer. We must follow a gradual and progressive approach in bed, but more importantly, we must learn to continually seduce her throughout the day: whisper tender words in her ear, hold her tightly, pamper her and caress her, so to prepare her to experience pleasure.

Men tend to get fixated with the sexual organ, thinking it's is the only path to the promise land. They forget that the most substantial sense organ in a woman's body is her skin, and that every part of her body is capable of absorbing pleasure. A woman's body consists of a vast neurological infrastructure that absorbs and transports pleasure signals throughout her body. If there are tensions anywhere, it will block the pleasure signal from circulating. Therefore, learn how to massage her and release muscular tensions, so they don't abrupt sensory signals from circulating, and learn how to kiss her and caress her, so to open up all her neurological pleasure centers.

If you can wake up her pleasure centers, you will expand her sexual pleasure to reach beyond the minute geographical location of her sexual organ and encapsulate her entire body. It will amplify and circulate until her whole body is enraptured in pleasure and enjoyment.

There are certainly things to be discussed regarding where and how to touch a woman in order to stimulate her entire neurological system, and we will discuss it further later in the book. However, the stimulation of her body is merely subsidiary to the true key to sexual fulfilment. Well beyond bodily caresses, it is the stimulation of her mind that opens the path to supreme ecstasy.

A woman's ability to experience orgasmic sensations is only mildly associated with the stimulation of her body. It is her mind that prepares her to release euphoric chemicals. If there are suppressed traumas in her mind, such as fear, low self-esteem, and unresolved conflicts, it will keep her from producing the fluids and chemicals necessary to experience pleasure. It doesn't matter what you do to her body. You can try all the positions and techniques you learned from your tantra book, but it will have no effect. You must learn to stimulate her mind. You must be able to awaken her to the soft treasures buried within her heart. You must speak to her inner desires and satisfy the deep yearnings in her heart. Wisper words of affection in her ears, instill her with yearning for your touch, and spark her deepest desires. But beyond words, you must become a man worthy of her surrender. If she can surrender to your love, the cosmic intelligence will do its work. Her body will naturally begin to respond, and earthshattering sensations will start to bubble inside her body.

The orgasm is an amazing phenomenon. For those few moments you float in a timeless, formless, blissful void. There are no thoughts, no worries, no emotions. Nothing, and no one else matters in that moment. We experience something beyond the language of our physical world, pure ecstasy and spiritual bliss.

As men, we tend to agglomerate the orgasm and the ejaculation as the same phenomena, when in truth they are separate. Ejaculation is the physical release of bodily fluids, but the orgasm is a deep spiritual phenomenon. It is linked to the fulfilment of a cosmic principle. As men we can experience multiple orgasms during lovemaking, independent of ejaculation, but it requires that we train ourselves to disassociate orgasms and ejaculations. Likewise, a woman is capable of floating in ecstasy for an enduring length of time. If we investigate the depths of sexual fulfillment, we will find no end. It can only be compared to the pure elixir of eternal life.

It is this knowledge that sexual stimulation happens in the mind and the spirit, that convinces us that supreme sexual fulfillment can only be reached in a committed relationship. When a girl gets laid only one night, she ends up doubting her own value and beauty. She might cry herself to sleep wondering what is wrong with her, and eventually lose trust in everything including herself. This gives birth to a low self-esteem that stimulates envy, jealousy, rage, depression, fear, insecurity, and all kinds of suppressed personal traumas. This is where mismanaged sexual energy becomes a generator of heart brakes or even criminal behavior in the long run if not healed.

These traumas get stored in our bodies, inhibiting our neurological infrastructure, making us incapable of experiencing the true depth of sexual fulfillment. Don't waste your sexual energy on self-stimulation or arbitrary encounters. Doing so will eventually drain your life-force and rob you from true lasting fulfilment.

Making love often in a healthy committed relationship is one of the greatest benefactors for our universal health. It involves exercise of the heart, the mind and the spirit. It can cure ailments such as: heart problems, mental health conditions, prostate or breasts cancer, menstrual cramps, stress, insomnia, incontinence, muscle or joints overload. It promotes shinny skin as we discard toxins during perspiration, it aids our memory, our mood, our immune system, our heart, and our balance.

Sex can have tremendous effects on our health, but it can also bring total destruction. Careless sexual indulgence can give rise to dreadful mental, spiritual and physical diseases. The difference lies in our abilities to cultivate a lifegiving and uplifting sexual bond that harmonizes with natures principles. What we need is a legitimate, guiltless, intimate and enriched sexual communion.

Closing Remarks

Men have continuously pondered the mysteries of women's desires since ancient times. However, as we have discovered, unlocking the doors to a woman's heart is not so mysterious. Satisfying a woman's yearnings requires that we dive into her unspoken needs. We must realize that the irrational behavior that make men bewildered are a natural result of primordial needs being unfulfilled. When we satisfy her deepest longings, her true nature begins to sprout, and suddenly she becomes far less bewildering.

We must be dedicated and wise to love a woman. She is like a flower that requires adoration, care and nourishment. If you fail to cherish her, the flame of her feminine spirit will soon wither. Eventually you will no longer recognize the woman you once fell in love with. Reversely, if you make her feel beautiful, and take time to spark and nurture the divinity within her, then you'll gain the power to transform her into the woman of your dreams. Love is ultimately a journey, an ongoing dance between two people, and you must continually invest to keep it alive. If you are wise and true, you can bring life to the greatest marvel in human life, the second great blessing, endowed at the dawn of human history.

Harmony

Chapter 5

«The highest education is that which does not merely give us information but makes our life in harmony with all existence. »

~Rabindranath Tagore

An essential ingredient in a loving relationship is harmony. Unfortunately, harmonizing two vastly different elements is an intricate matter, isn't it? So how do two tango? How do we go from disparity to synchronicity? It requires a dedicated effort from each partner, but it also requires a healthy dose of wisdom. This chapter will discuss the mindsets and tactics that provide harmony in a relationship.

Let Her Win

All my life I have been fiercely passionate about games and competitions. My cultural roots are pure Viking, and the Viking kings awarded positions of authority to those who could dominate others through brute force during competitions. If you didn't fight to win without regard for the shedding of blood, you were branded as a weakling and an outcast. This culture lives on, although quietly, within me and my countrymen.

My best friend moved into the house next to ours when we were 8 years old, and we grew up competing at every possible game we could find, and when we got bored of those, we invented new games to compete at. We would decide on a new discipline and spend the next two weeks training like maniacs before our final showdown. These battles were always dead serious, almost to the point of damaging our relationship.

Because of this experience I developed many skills helpful for all kinds of competition. The irony is that this kind of winner-take-all, all-out fight-to-the-death approach to life is in the end a failed strategy. People resent you if you stomp all over them just for fun. How much more they resent you if you try to dominate them in areas that are important and have long-term consequences for their well-being. I have come to learn that the true victor is not the champion by the sword, but rather the sage who extends the olive branch.

Due to my background, it took me a long time to realize that in relationships you can't win from winning. You can only gain ground by distancing yourself from the concept of winning or losing, and by finding the way to walk in harmony with your partner. So often we go all out to win an argument, all noble and in the pursuit of truth, and in the end all we've done is alienated the people we care about. What can anyone win if we can't even hear each other with respect? The real opportunity of this kind of exchange is the chance to broaden our understanding and to reach out to embrace the "other." If you are the man who always must be right, then you will be the man who always ends up alone.

If you really want to influence people, then focus on building relationships. This is the true key to influence and happiness. I learned the reality of this while working in sales. At first, I thought that winning the sale was everything. So naturally I pushed my clients so hard that they felt forced to make the purchase. Very often I won, and I made high sales numbers. However, I quickly noticed that it got harder and harder to win sales. Almost all my clients made only one purchase, and then they never wanted to hear from our company again. Naturally I had to change my tactics. Rather than trying to win, I decided to try my best to let my client win.

I worked to offer the best possible product fitting his needs at the best possible price. What did I have to lose? Of course, it wounded my pride that I would often lose the sale, and my sales results went down considerably. Over time however, the sales of our company skyrocketed. More and more customers wanted to buy from us, and they told their friends how great we were. New customers streamed in, and we reached the highest sales numbers we had ever attained.

The greatest thing for me, though, was that I felt much better about myself when I changed my tactics. I had a clean conscience and it provided me with a newfound energy to serve my clients.

As I applied this method of "losing" to other areas of my life, I soon noticed that my quality of life wasn't affected so much by winning or losing after all, but rather by the mindset by which I acted. Men are hardwired to try to win at everything, but most of our goals in life are achieved by building and maintaining relationships. Women generally know this and are usually far less competitive. This is why sports generally mean less to women than to men. Women can therefore feel hurt if you "shoot to kill" in an argument or even a game with them. You will end up a much happier man if you sacrifice your pride or the need to be right and let her win. You can win her to your viewpoint over time, gently, kindly, instead of dominating a discussion to prove beyond doubt how wrong or even foolish she has been.

There are certainly times in our lives where we must exert our every ounce of power to gain victory, but there are other times were "losing" can provide a more beneficial result. In fact, most of our interactions belong to the second category. If you're in a debate, then take a moment to consider your intentions for persuading the other person. Are you trying to help them, or are you merely trying to display your dominance? Consider if there are more important issues at hand. If you let them win, chances are they will be more open to hearing you out on a more important issue.

People have so many different views, talents, experiences, and insights. Learning to navigate our relationships is like composing a great symphony. You must know which instrument should play solo at which time, which part of the melody needs which kind of harmony. Our lives become like masterpieces when we can maintain a perspective infused with love, sensitive to the overarching purpose and joy that make life precious.

Apologize and Forgive

Even if we strive to live in perfect harmony, we will eventually fall prey to our imperfect nature. This is inevitable. The saving grace comes from our abilities to deftly apologize for our mistakes and forgive others for theirs. For this reason, it is imperative that we learn and practice these skills.

There is a famous story in the Old Testament about Adam and Eve falling in the Garden of Eden after having eaten from the forbidden Tree of Knowledge of Good and Evil. Allegedly this act initiated a spiral that ultimately separated man from God. This story has been perpetuated in various forms through a wide range of cultures and religions. The peculiar observation made from reading these stories is that the primordial beings never repented for their mistakes. If they stopped blaming each other, humbly plead for forgiveness, promised absolute faithfulness, and thereafter displayed tangible evidence of their sincerity, would history have progressed any differently?

In a parallel story, King David killed the man of the woman he was committing adultery with. You could easily say that his sin was greater. However, David had a special attribute that made him worthy of his kingship. He possessed the adroit ability to sincerely repent and apologize. For instance, when a man cursed him and threw rocks at him, he said to his guards: "If the Lord has told him to curse me, then who are you to tell him to stop?" It was this special ability that led to his forgiveness, justification and glorification.

I am certainly not using this example as a theology lesson, but as an example of the power of humility and repentance, of how pride can destroy a relationship no matter how sanctified, and of how sincere repentance can salvage the direst situation. Ask yourself the question, would you forgive your children if they approached you with sincere humble apologies? Would you forgive your friend or your spouse?

Conflicts typically arise because of a glorification of justice. "Justice must be served!" they proclaim, "Otherwise there will be no reconciliation!" What foolishness. When we get obsessed with justice, we tend to expect the person at fault to apologize first. Problems then occurs when both parties believe the other person is at fault, which, of course, encapsulates nearly all conflicts.

Our minds are brilliant at camouflaging our responsibility and at fabricating excuses or justifications for our behaviors; especially if it is programmed that way through consistent and stubborn lack of repentance. We subconsciously forge a reality that makes us blameless, and we are thus blinded from the opportunity to reconcile. Only a truly wise person can pierce through this forged reality and repent, even when he feels blameless. Most people wait for the feeling of guilt to kick in before they apologize, but these feelings usually come after you break your inner justifications. We must sacrifice our pride first, only then will we see a higher perspective.

Most people's response to a conflict is to first scan their minds for justifications for their behaviors. Next, they scan the other persons behavior to discover their flaws. Harmony calls us to consider an alternative approach. Let's abandon the other persons involvement, and instead search for our own faults. If we sincerely seek our minds, free from pride, we will often discover ways we could have behaved differently.

Even if we find no faults within ourselves, we should learn to apologize. Instead of considering apologies as a tool for justice, consider it a tool for reconciliation, and use it to restore harmony whenever someone is upset with you. By training our minds to consistently embrace a higher perspective, we will take substantial strides in our abilities to rebuild relationships and resolve conflicts.

The second step is learning how to apologize properly. You can do it the wrong way like this: "Okay, I'm sorry, Okay!? I said I'm sorry!" Or the right way: "Baby, I'm sorry. I'm really, really sorry... I didn't mean to make you feel the way you feel right now. I promise it will never happen again."

Then, with stretched open arms, you whisper with a firm but tender voice: "Come here baby." Once in your arms, you hold her face in your hands and kiss her tenderly on her cheeks, forehead, lips, etc., and ask under your breath: "Hey, am I forgiven?" Even if the answer is no, keep your ground, your dignity, and your affectionate approach. Comfort her and say: "I'll do anything in my power to make it up to you."

Conflicts are inevitable in any relationship, and if we are unwise, they can shatter us beyond repair. However, if we are wise, then conflicts can be steppingstones to enhance our intimacy. Yes, it's true. Facing a conflict offers the opportunity to deepen our connection with someone. If we learn to master the skill of repentance and apologies, we can use it to create heartfelt reconciliation in the face of fierce conflict. Then, oftentimes, our connection will grow deeper than if the conflict never happened.

In addition to learning how to apologize, we must learn to forgive. People feel a sense of power attached to withholding their forgiveness. They consider it a sacred jewel that they can't offer up too easily. They forget that harboring resentment effects themselves far more than the object of their resentment. Nelson Mandela said that "Keeping resentment is like drinking poison hoping that the other person would die." It hurts others, but it hurts us more by poisoning our minds with depressive and destructive thoughts. Forgiveness can be difficult, but it is a necessary skill to develop.

The best way to forgive is to access our empathy and step into the other persons shoes. Realize the pain they went through that led them to think or behave the way they do. If we can dive into their reality, we are able to develop compassion. With compassion we will have mercy; with mercy we can forgive.

When you forgive, forget that you forgave. Of course, you must learn so to not make the same mistakes, but don't hold the past against others. If someone has repented and promised to change, trust them with high expectancies. If you expect them to fail you in the future, they most certainly will. If you trust that they won't then of course they still may, but this is still a better method.

The Way of Jacob

I would like to summarize the section on apologies and forgiveness by sharing the story of someone who has truly mastered these skills. The story of Jacob offers one of the most aptly displays of the power of repentance.

There are two stories in the Old Testament concerning the conflicts between a younger and older brother: the story of Jacob and Esau, and the story of Cain and Abel. In one story the younger brother ends up killed, in the other story the brothers are reconciled. Some people might make the claim that the difference in these stories is between the older brothers, Cain and Esau, but I want to make the claim that it was the special abilities of Jacob that made all the difference.

In the story, Jacob was able to acquire the birthright after exchanging it with some food from his starving brother, and then tricking his blind father with the aid of his mother. You could say that Jacob tricked his brother and his father illegitimately, but from another perspective, you could say that Jacob bought the birthright fair and square, and then obeyed his mother's will to receive the birthright from his father. Most of us would likely forge a reality in our minds like the second perspective, to make ourselves blameless. It would be completely natural for Jacob to do the same, but as we will see; he didn't.

Following this, Jacob left his homeland in order to work for his uncle in a foreign land. In other words, he left his inheritance and decided to work for his own blessings. Jacob lived a rough life for twenty-one years to acquire wealth and a family after being tricked by his uncle. Then he went, according to the story, to wrestle with an angel who broke his hip. He finally returned home exhausted and broken to reconcile with his brother.

Jacob knew that going home meant certain death because his brother had assembled an army of people to kill him. Still, his love for his brother compelled him to reconcile. He approached his brother utterly exhausted after his battle with the angel, but rather than fighting or fleeing, he kneeled down in front of him, and sincerely pleaded for forgiveness. He offered him his life, his wealth and his family, and said to his brother, the man about to kill him: "In you I see the face of God." He did this even though from a very reasonable perspective he was blameless. His brother melted, put down his swords, and embraced him.

Jesus Christ said that if you are about to make an offering and remember that your brother has something against you, leave your offering and reconcile with your brother. Once forgiven, go back to make your offering. We don't know much about what Abel did to reconcile with, encourage, or help his brother. The story doesn't elaborate. But whatever he did, it was enough to provoke Cain to kill him. So, the moral of the story is: Don't be like Abel, be like Jacob. Assume responsibility for your brother's resentment, whether it is justified in your eyes or not.

Abel may have sacrificed his life for the sake of his pride, while Jacob sacrificed his pride for the sake of his life and the reconciliation with his brother. Resentment has the power to drain our spirits. This is true whether you are on the sending or receiving end of it. Therefore, if you have a dispute, drop what you are doing and seek to reconcile. Otherwise you will continue to dwell in conflict, unable to be productive, or worse: you will perish.

Humility

It is becoming more and more evident to me that pride sabotages harmony. As Solomon would say: "Pride goes before destruction." If you want to have good relationships, you need to embrace humility.

To some people this is simple, but for others it's nearly impossible. I am afraid I'm in the second category. Growing up I always got the best grades in school and learned new things quickly. Without my even realizing it consciously, I took the attitude, "Hey, I'm great at sports, great at school, and I know almost everything that's important to know. I really am all that." I feigned humility, and even convinced myself, but there was still a confidence in my heart that I was superior as a human being. What a foolish boy I was.

The only way to overcome arrogance is to realize the truth. The truth is that our value is not determined by our abilities, gifts, or accomplishments, but rather by our birthright. We have inherited two great gifts at birth. First, we have been given the gift of life. The most important assets we will ever acquire cannot compare to the ones bestowed to us at birth: our ears, our eyes, our pounding hearts. Who would ever exchange their eyes or limbs for money or fame?

Our second great inheritance is our potential to love. Every person born on earth has this amazing attribute, although we may have different life experiences that support us or hinder us from fulfilling that potential. Some people are born into homes rich with love and provisions, others are born in difficult or even tragic circumstances. But each of us has the irrepressible destiny to give and receive love, and each of us has the potential to become a virtuoso in the art of loving. The purpose of life on earth, and even beyond this lifetime, is to develop our capacity to love.

These two great gifts, given freely to all human beings, make other talents seem pale, and so we find ourselves humbled by the fact that we are all indebted to something greater than ourselves for our own resplendent nature. But another cause for humility, is that we can't develop any of our talents, or even live out our lives, except by receiving our life and breath from the earth and sky. Our very flesh sprang from our mother's body, and the fruits of the earth nourished us from day one. Anything we know or have accomplished leaves us indebted to our teachers and our mentors. If you see things for what they are, pride is very silly. Of course, there is a kind of pride that is important for us, a pride in the fact that we have chosen well or invested sincere work in a worthy task. But the foundation for that kind of pride can only be gratitude and humility in the face of all that we have received.

Maturity

Inherent to the role of a man is the ability to provide security, stability, strength, presence and constancy to his home. Therefore, it's essential for us to mature into men capable of embracing these sacred responsibilities. For our families to blossom, we need the maturity to put their needs before our own, and the strength of character to face the challenges that come to us all in life.

What does it mean to be mature? The mark of a mature tree is that it bears fruits or flowers. In other words, maturity involves switching your focus from your own development to the development of new life around you. For a tree to bear good fruit, its roots must be deep and firmly planted in the ground and the trunk must be strong enough to carry the extra weight. Our roots are our core principles and values, and the strength of our trunk is determined by our discipline, willpower, and character. When you can care for yourself, you're independent. When you can care for others as well, then you're mature.

Consider the Needs of Others

What are the first thoughts that come to your mind when you wake up in the morning? "What should I eat for breakfast? What should I do today to be happy? How can I maximize my profit from this day?" Or do you consider your spouse first? "What does she need from me today? How can I ensure her happiness and wellbeing?" A man's thoughts when he first wakes up in the morning says a lot about his character.

Many people feel justified in ensuring their own happiness and leaving it to others to care about theirs. However, living only for your own sake can only be justified if you never received anything from others. Can anyone honestly say their lives are debt-free? As a child, who fed you, clothed you and changed your diapers? Who paid for your school supplies? Who mentored you, and instilled in you your values and principles? Who provided you with your eyes and ears, and legs and arms? Who provides you with oxygen, sunlight, and natural beauty as far as the eyes can see? Who built your civilization? Who ensured your safety from foreign and domestic invasion? When we start asking these types of questions, we quickly realize that we are infinitely indebted to the environment around us. We must live our lives in an attempt to repay these debts. True justice can only be found in the service of others.

Beyond Justice, this is where true happiness is found. You may be a brilliant virtuoso but singing to yourself will never make you happy. There is no happiness unless you share your gifts with others. Even the humblest or most trivial gesture or gift can bring you happiness when you share it with another. This is the true secret to happiness.

Don't Complain

Words are magic. They have the power to attract invisible and even tangible elements that affect the quality of your life and the lives of those around you. Therefore, make sure your language is inspiring and uplifting, free from despondency and doubt.

A man's complaints reveal the quality of his character. If he grumbles over small things, it speaks to his vision and moral standard. Complaining has the power to puncture your spirit and make you weak. It draws you to the lesser things in life and blinds you from finding solutions. It also makes you appear selfish and ungrateful. It makes your girl feel unsafe, confused, and think that there is something wrong with her. It might even make her doubt your love for her, and damage her self-worth, because the joy you share is unable to overshadow the things you complain about. Ultimately, she might lose trust in you, because you appear incapable of handling your problems in silence.

Be firm with yourself when it comes to complaining. Catch yourself before you speak and remind yourself of the damages your words can cause. Value and protect your dignity and self-confidence by refusing to surrender to your complaints. Refuse to give in, no matter how tempting it might sound in a moment of frustration. Practice looking at challenges as opportunities rather than problems and realize that solutions are found in the inner resources provided by a calm and inspired state of mind. If you can maintain this mental discipline, your beloved will draw inspiration from you and feel indebted to your courage in the face of difficulty.

Feel free to confide in your girl before making decisions. Sharing your concerns are entirely different from complaining. Complaining is generally a refusal to accept responsibility, it typically includes blaming others for your problems, or lashing out about the unfairness of life. Confiding in others and asking for advice and support is a sign of wisdom, but ultimately, you must take responsibility to overcome your own challenges.

<u>Don't Get Offended</u>

Our society has a peculiar strategy for raising children. I once brought my daughter to a childcare and watched the kids play. I kept hearing the adults yell: "Jackson! Jackson!!" Apparently, a little boy named Jackson kept making trouble by pushing the other kids and steeling their toys, etc. The adults quickly ran to comfort the children who were whining, and they kept chastising Jackson for his antics. It made me realize that our society is training people to be offended, by offering attention and comfort to whoever cries the loudest.

In addition to educating the kids who are offensive, we should educate those who get offended. Train them that it's okay if someone snatches your toy, or pushes you, or calls you names. Chances are there are plenty of other toys to play with, chances are you will survive your little bruise, and chances are there is a hint of truth to their name calling. Disharmony doesn't generally happen because people are offensive. Offences are an inevitable reality of life that happens with or without malicious intent. True conflict arises because people get offended and feel the need to retaliate.

There are countless reasons to be offended these days. People say outlandish things all the time. However, don't be shaken.   If something drives you crazy on the other side of the world, that you can't do anything about, don't let it destabilize you. Of course, if you believe injustice has been done, and you can do something about it, then by all means pursue it boldly. But if not, then the wisest thing is to send a prayer or a positive thought to the people involved, and let it go.

If someone attacks you directly, listen humbly and accept any criticism that comes your way. And if something a little unpleasant happens, don't let it get you down. If you get offended because someone addresses you with the wrong title, challenges your beliefs, overcharges you by a few dollars, beats you to a parking spot, dislikes your shoes or thinks you suck at tennis, then what does that say about your character?

It doesn't feel right for us to freak out over a parking space, especially considering that many people face truly severe problems every day. Stop to think for a moment about the harsh realities of violent crime, child starvation, or even deadly deceases. Let these cold truths wake you up and push you to maintain a responsible and balanced attitude. Control yourself when little things go wrong, and you'll find that your relationship and all your affairs proceed more smoothly.

In an intimate relationship, there are plenty of opportunities to offend each other. Maybe your girl is upset, maybe she's worried about you, maybe she's trying to protect you, maybe she just has a way of speaking that gets on your nerves, or maybe she's deliberately trying to upset you, just to see what you're made of. In times like these, take a deep breath and gaze at her. Turn off the sounds of her voice in your mind for a minute as you look into her eyes. Remember the big picture, forget about your pride, and remember that offences are nothing but soft dew that evaporates in the wind if you don't engage them.

If you can't resist the temptation to engage with offences and fly off the handle, raise your voice and join the fray, you can tear the fabric of your relationship in ways that aren't easily mended. Especially if freaking out is your "go to" response. Instead, accept what she tells you, speak to her from your compassion and humility, and comfort her frustration. Build up your self-confidence and transcend your ego. This way, offences will have no power over you.

Don't Fear Rejection

If you play a sport, then you know what it's like to be picked last. If you ask questions of your teachers or employers, then you know what it's like when they brush you off and make you look foolish. If you approached an attractive girl, you may have felt the dread of rejection. Some people avoid these unpleasant experiences by keeping out of sight, afraid to approach the world as their true authentic selves. Rejection is a natural part of life. It isn't necessary for every person to like you. What matters is that you're worthy of self-respect and the respect and love of those dearest to you.

It is hard to respect a man who lacks dignity and self-love, and who looks for validation from others. He is hard to trust, because you don't know whether he speaks from his authentic heart or based on what he believes you want to hear. He is manipulable and unreliable, because his decisions are based on other people's opinions instead of his core values.

Don't fear rejections. Instead become a man of integrity. Think through your values and keep your convictions as your compass and ballast. Do good because it naturally springs from the desires in your heart. This way you will attract the right kind of people into your life.

If someone rejects you, use your values and principles as your guide. Is their rejection justifiable? Can you learn something from their criticism? If so, use the rejection as a valuable life lesson. Don't take rejections to heart, or shy away or retaliate because someone rejects you initially. A man who can continue to love people despite repeated rejections can break through any wall. He can reach any person, accomplish any dream, and melt his lady's heart.

Don't Give Up

Don't let life's challenges keep you down. Unexpected hardships inevitably occur. You might be struck by a sudden sickness, financial difficulty, or emotional trauma, but don't let it overwhelm you. Digest your situation for a short while, and then use your trials as springboards for your future success. Train your mind to see opportunities and possibilities in the face of difficulty, and always strive to move forward with a courageous attitude.

The road to victory is paved by hardship and difficulty, so do not give up when they strike. Obstacles are a necessary part of your journey, because they strengthen your character and forces you to access your deep inner resources. If you persist, you can eventually overcome any obstacle. Think about the qualities of water. Water is yielding and supple, but because of its persistence in traveling down the mountain, it can overcome any obstacle. When faced with an obstruction, it finds its way over or around, and eventually carves down solid rock. So, in the famous words of Bruce Lee: "be water, my friend."

Just as you should not give up on yourself, you should not give up on others, especially the love of your life. If your beloved knows that you will never give up on her despite her flaws, she will have the courage and emotional support to get through hard times. She will be able to seek sanctuary in your understanding and solace in your arms. It is not the trials that disrupt our harmony, but our lack of faith, courage and persistence to overcome them.

Generosity

My Rwandese friend once told me a story of the missionaries who came to her hometown after the tragic genocide of the 1990's. She explained that the director of the food program counted every portion of every meal with a meticulous and grave attitude. My friend and the other locals became worried for this lady, thinking she must be terribly poor to fuss over every grain of rice. They decided to take up a collection of food from friends and neighbors to help the poor woman. After some time, however, they realized that she wasn't poor at all! At least not materially. She had plenty, but her mind reduced it all to poverty and lack. Unfortunately, stinginess is common among westerners and it is detrimental to our relationships. It's not the money or the resources that matters, but rather our ability to make our stuff less important to us than our loved ones.

Generosity is a lost virtue in western society, due to the glorification of individualism. Although we are the wealthiest people on earth, we are also the stingiest. How ironic! In third world countries, people may have less, but they share freely, so their culture is rich in warmth and love. They do not generally consider their wealth a result of personal fortune or hard work, but rather as a blessing. Naturally, they are more inclined to share what little they have with others.

Is it possible to buy someone's affection? Of course, it is! I highly recommend it. But it's not the money that makes the purchase in the end. The affection is awarded because of the heart of giving.

The Gospel of Mark tells the story of the widow's mite. Jesus watched many people put money into the treasury, some of whom put in much. Then one poor woman put in two small coins. Jesus told his disciples: "Assuredly I say to you that this poor widow has put in more than all those who have given to the treasury; for all they put in out of their abundance, but she out of her poverty." (Mark 12:42-44). Similarly, your partner may not be impressed merely by the amount you give her, but by your sincerity and love for her. If you have much, give much. If you have little, give from what you have. But in any case, give well, with joy and affection.

Spoil her as much as you can, not just when you are winning her, but even once you know that she is yours. Buy her jewelry, nice clothes, or flowers every once in a while. Take her out shopping and let her buy whatever she wants, even if she makes more money than you. Help her choose clothes that make her feel like a beauty. Don't be afraid to spend a few dollars now and then. Making your woman feel that she is precious to you is a better buy than most of the ways you could let go of your money.

If you have a genuine concern about your expenses, it's okay to tell her. Say something like: "You know I want to buy you the whole world. I want you to feel like a princess whenever you are with me. However, I am worried about our financial future together if I keep spending so much. Would you remind me about this sometimes? It's hard for me to be careful about it when I'm with you." If you tell her this way, then she will most certainly understand, provided you have a habit of generosity. Many women will be able to feel your heart without your having to say anything. Many will be happy to help you to be moderate and responsible.

Generosity is about more than giving money. Be generous also with your heart and time. If someone needs your help, offer it to them, free of charge. If someone needs your love or attention, then be there for them. Develop a habit of generosity and the mindset of living for the sake of others. When you consider your blessings as an opportunity to bless others, then your capacity to love increases immeasurably.

Loving Her Family

There is a peculiar culture in the west, perhaps an unwritten law, that a husband and wife should despise their mother in-laws. This norm becomes a driving force for family breakdown.

When you only have your wife to consider, and perhaps you start to realize you don't really like her much anymore, it seems an easy solution to file for divorce. However, if divorce means severing half your family, it suddenly becomes far more complicated, and your heart may compel you to work out your problems and mend what is broken.

When you take a lady to be yours, you should embrace all of her, and consider her entire family to be yours. You should consider her mother and father to be as important to you as your own mother and father and dedicate yourself to loving them and serving them faithfully. Her brothers and sisters (and close friends) should be like your own brothers and sisters too, and they should be able to rely on you as their own brother. This way, your in-laws become a glue for your relationship during hard times, rather than a cleaver that helps tear it apart.

Of course, you don't reach this level of trust automatically, it requires effort, so make it your mission to win their hearts, just as you won your darlings heart. Likewise, you should teach her to consider your family her own, and arduously work to bring them close together.

No one knows your lady's heart, needs and longings, better than her family, and if you can win their trust, they will become your best resource for understanding her. As you interact with them, you will come to know her in a whole new light, and If you struggle in your relationship, they will give you answers. Ideally, you should reach a point where her family cares more about your day to day happiness, then their own daughter's. A mother in-law can perhaps not scold her son in-law for not loving her daughter well, but she can certainly educate her daughter if she sees your needs are unfulfilled. Likewise, if your family is close to your wife, then they will be invested in her wellbeing, and offer you invaluable guidelines to treating her right.

If you love her family like your own, and if your family loves her like their own, it will bring your girl a whole new level of assurance and trust in your relationship. Her heart will begin to sprout knowing that you have not stolen her from her family, but rather embraced them as your own. Additionally, she will have gained a whole new family through yours.

When you take a woman to be yours, you not only receive her into your loving care, but all the people important to her life. An essential part of ensuring harmony, stability and happiness in your relationship, is therefore to invest in her family and friends.

Closing Thoughts

Harmony requires wisdom, candid presence, eloquence, selflessness, and occasional cunningness. We must establish our core values and develop our emotional discipline so to not give rise to destructive conflict. We must consider the needs of others and live our lives in humility and gratitude for all we have received. If we can develop the wisdom of Jacob, we can melt the fiercest and stingiest soul, and spread harmony and color in our wake. From a place of harmony, we can plant seeds that blossom into brilliant expressions of joy and intimacy.

Beauty

Chapter 6

«There are only two ways to live your life: as though nothing is a miracle, or as though everything is»

~Albert Einstein (Apocryphal)

You are looking at a piece of paper with straight and curved black lines all over it, aren't you? You may wonder how I know this; it's because you and I are at this very moment sharing in the magic of the written word. But what about the magic of the straight and curved elements brimming with life all around us? What about the fact that every entity, living or inanimate, is eloquent in form, from its tiny nuclei all the way to its many-faceted and various qualities? Can we see the loveliness and meaning that shines in everything that exists?

When you appreciate beauty, then the places, events, and even people that may have seemed dull suddenly hold your fascination. This change in perception transfigures your experience, and you in turn revitalize the people you engage throughout the day. When we identify beauty, we can draw it out in others. If you practice seeing the world, and especially other people, with the eyes of love, then the people around you will feel renewed. You will have seen something inherent within them, given them permission to shine.

This way of seeing has special meaning within an intimate, committed relationship, because the process of discovering your beloved's inherent beauty is an eternal adventure, like finding the edge of the universe. As you go deeper into your love for her, you can build a unique appreciation of your lady's beauty that enhances your union until your love is unbreakable. Wherever we are, whatever we're doing, mindfulness of beauty is the difference between experiencing mere marks on a page and living encompassed by eloquence quivering in the air, yet undiscovered around every bend along the way.

What is Beauty?

What is the measurement of beauty? Weight, height, volume, BTUs, lumens? No, beauty is a measure of the emotional response it stimulates in its observer. Beauty is not its own independent attribute. It exists as part of a relationship. A rose is beautiful if someone stops to admire it, to marvel at its vibrant colors and to smell its delicious perfumes. Without an observer, beauty is never actualized. Considering this, we must understand that we have tremendous abilities to instill beauty in an object.

Your gaze is your greatest gift to your beloved, because it has the power to bring life to her glorious feminine attributes. If she continuously catches you gazing at her with tenderness in your heart, when your words and gestures reflect your adoration, and when your arms are open to receive her inner beauty, you will see her radiance emerge from within. On the other hand, if you are asleep to her beauty, it will remain dormant and never surface nor blossom. A man who says his woman lacks beauty must therefore admit to having failed her.

Let's pause and ponder the real meaning of beauty. Our concepts of beauty are shaped by the unscrupulous media empires that churn out images of skeleton thin youths in scant clothing, looking as if they are dying of boredom as well as starvation. These beauty standards undergo radical changes every decade or so. 50 years ago, women were supposed to be fat, 30 years ago they were supposed to be skinny, then they were supposed to be curvy again. Small breasts, big breasts, big butts, small butts, medium sized butts, it is constantly changing. So, let's not rely on our rather bizarre culture to teach us about beauty. Let's look a bit deeper.

Philosophers have theorized about what makes something beautiful. They cite elements like symmetry and proportion. But more than the qualities of the object in our gaze, it is our perception that instills beauty. Beauty exists where we expect it to be, and something that is continuously adored achieves the peace necessary for its beauty to blossom.

A great illustration of this principle is found in the famous experiment conducted by the Japanese scientist Dr. Masaru Emoto. He documented the effect of our thoughts on water as it crystallizes into ice. In the experiments he exposed water molecules to beautiful music and kind words while freezing them. He then studied the ice crystals through a microscope. The crystals had pleasing patterns and were clear and symmetrical. Next, he exposed the molecules to frenetic music and hostile words. The frozen shapes were ugly and hellish, painful to look at. Search for his video "Water, Consciousness and Intent" to see the images for yourself. If our thoughts have such powerful effects on ice crystals, imagine the effects on a woman in response to her devoted lover.

Discovering Beauty

I would like to share with you the story that shaped my perception of beauty. Perhaps it will open a window to splendor for you as it did for me.

People travel from the four corners of the earth to visit my hometown because of its unparalleled natural beauty. As a kid, though, I was never able to appreciate it. My father would take me to explore our famous fjords every summer. He would show me the great Pulpit Rock, the Hardanger Fjord, and countless breathtaking waterfalls and majestic glaciers. But at the time I could not understand what all the fuss was about. All I could see were water and rocks, and I was bored out of my mind! It was not until years later that I could see these marvels for what they are, not until after I met a young Japanese lady in Montego Bay.

I was about twenty years old and had been in Jamaica for about two weeks at the time. I had already seen the major sites. I had seen the Bob Marley museum in Kingston, the blue lagoon in Port Antonio, and I had even climbed the Dungeon Waterfall in Ocho Rios. I was not particularly impressed. I was just as bored as I was at home. But then one day a young Japanese lady, named Yui, walked into our hostel.

We ended up talking for about an hour, and as I listened to her adventures from all around the world, I felt that there was something different about her. Her eyes had a sparkle, and her stories drew me irresistibly in, even though I'd heard so many similar stories before. I wondered what had given her the fire, the passion for life that was so evident in her shining face and animated voice.

I invited her to join me for a trip to the Martha Brae River. I was a bit reluctant to ask her to come along, thinking that she would be bored on such a small, local trip after all the beautiful and famous places she had been to. But she accepted my invitation, and the next day we were starting down the river on our primitive little raft made from bamboo logs and rope. The water was completely green, filled with vegetation and wild creatures, everything from insects to river turtles. To me it looked more like a swamp, and I must admit, I was slightly disgusted. My friend on the other hand was so busy taking pictures of everything that I could hardly get her attention.

We approached a small spring, with waters streaming from a crack in the rocks. Our guide told us it came all the way from the top of the river, and it was the purest water in Jamaica. When my friend filled up her cup and drank the fresh water, her face began to shine and her whole body seemed to relax. I took some as well, but to me it tasted ordinary, I began to see that she was having a completely different experience from mine because she was choosing to see things differently. I couldn't believe how excited she got over a cup of water!

As we floated on, we passed a little swing made from rope and a tractor wheel, and ahead I could see some log houses selling refreshments and souvenirs. I was just salivating at the thought of soda when Yui's camera fell into my lap! And there she was, splashing through the water to the little swing. I yelled at her, asking what the heck she was doing, but she just teased me with her adorable eyes, inviting me to join her for a swim.

Part of me was thinking, "There is no way I'm going into that green water. I don't know what ugly sea creatures and diseased fish live in there, and I sure don't want to find out!" But she looked so content with herself. (Well actually she reminded me of Smeagol from the lagoon scene in *Lord of the Rings*, although she was much prettier of course.) And aside from the lure of her childish delight, my curiosity got the better of me. Part of me couldn't resist my one chance to join her in her crazy beautiful world. I had to find out what all the fuss was about, and if I would ever understand, it would be now. As you've already guessed, I jumped.

What happened next really surprised me. I'll never forget it. From that moment until today, something has been different within me. To my shock, I discovered that I could see what Yui must have been seeing all along. With new eyes, I could recognize and feel how pristine and magical the lagoon was. I took a new look at the exotic Asian girl in front of me. She had shown me that it's all about the little things, all about the humble wonders. Her joy had infected me, and I would never be the same.

Suddenly, I felt the wind on my face as if for the first time. The little turtle struggling to get into the water from the bank, the hummingbirds near the shore, a big crab hiding its shell among the roots of a huge and alien-looking tree, I reveled in them all. The beauty of the forest unfolded before me in splendor that I had never been privy to before. My heart pumped faster, and adrenaline and serotonin flooded into my bloodstream. How exhilarating! How could I not have seen this before? Where had I been and what had I been doing during my twenty years on this planet?

When we finally arrived at the dock, alive to the unearthly beauty around me, I was suddenly overwhelmed by thoughts and mental snapshots of my hometown. From that distant island I caught my first real glimpse of the beauty of my motherland: the untouched nature, the spectacular mountains and shimmering fjords, wonder upon wonder as far the eyes can see. For the first time, I really missed home.

I'm so lucky that I met Yui. My experience with this extraordinary individual led me to a completely new way of seeing the world. Of course, the universe did not change. I changed. We have far more choice in how we experience life than we can easily imagine.

The Kingdom of Heaven

I once asked my spiritual master to describe the Kingdom of Heaven. He answered me, "It's differs little from the world you see here. The difference lies in the people, and their abilities to appreciate beauty. In the Kingdom of Heaven, you can look at a rock for a thousand years and not be bored. When your heart is filled with love, even the smallest thing is a wonder."

When we don't take time to open our hearts and savor the beauty around us, life becomes gloomy and dull. To fill our lives with splendor, we must choose to become mindful observers. We must take time to embrace the beauty around us, to savor the smells of the flowers, to eat our meals with awareness, and to truly notice the uniqueness of the people we meet. We tend to believe that the grass is greener elsewhere, but the truth is, our perceptions is what bring color to our reality. Choose to believe that nothing is more exciting than the day in front of you, the season you are in, the people in your life, and the girl by your side. Embrace the reality that life is awesome. Then you will find a newfound fascination for the events and people in your life, and people will be drawn to your enriched experience of life.

Train your ability to experience beauty. Get into the habit of picking up a tiny rock and study its magnificence. Feel its texture, its curves and edges, and observe its colors, shape and fragrance. Meditate on its history, the thousands of years it took to shape this little rock, all the forces it has been exposed to, and all the miles it has traveled to reach you. If you can find the beauty in this unique masterpiece, then you can learn to see it everywhere. Do this same exercise with flowers, trees, fruits and people. Do not compare one with another. Simply enjoy each item for what it is, exquisite and unique. When you can appreciate the beauty of nature's humble wonders, the beauty of your woman becomes infinitely more captivating. You will have developed the ability to cherish her, and with it, your ability to rekindle your passion and intimacy.

Our consumer society is founded on waste; things and people are bought, used, and thrown away. We think that if something doesn't suit our immediate pleasure then we can just throw it away and get something new. This mentality comes from a flawed perception. We think the flaws are found in the objects, when it is our perception that is flawed. Instead of blaming our environment, we should learn to instill and appreciate beauty, repent for our failure to nurture and raise up the people we love, and then get to work. This attitude will enable us to nourish a woman's latent inner beauty and spark new life into our relationships.

The Unexpected Gift

How do you feel when someone you love startles you with an unexpected gift? Let's see, there's a bit of anticipation, a bit of curiosity, and a major dose of childlike delight. Your heart dances with curiosity, and you can't wait to see what's beneath the wrapping!

What if I told you that every day is laden with these gifts? It is true if we recognize the gift within each moment and savor the feelings of mystery and anticipation. Learn to see your beloved as an unexpected gift and find within her the excitement of an unfolding fairy tale. Just as you light up when you unwrap a gift, light up in anticipation to the hidden mysteries contained in her heart. If you pay close attention, she can bestow you with beauties unknown.

Let this mindset give flavor to all your experiences with her. See every interaction as a gift. She may be sad, and offer you the gift of comforting her, or happy, and offer you the gift of sharing her joy. She may be frustrated and offer you the chance to listen. See her as a surprise gift from someone you love: as the sender and the gift itself. By seeing her this way, she will experience herself as truly precious. She will discover an adventurous and sacred connection to you, shaped and nourished by your ability to revel and appreciate her beauty.

When you look at your lady, practice extending your gaze beyond her eyes. Marvel at the beauty and softness of her lips, the shape of her nose, the color of her cheeks. Be responsive to her eyes, look to them to reveal her inner yearnings. Study the perfection and the artwork of her hair, listen to the music that her voice produces as she speaks, smell her fragrance, and marvel at her every curve. When you touch her, experience the fullness of her texture. Notice the feeling in your hand, as well as in your heart, as you caress her soft skin. Allow yourself to see her as if for the first time, with renewed innocence and curiosity. As you continue to shower her with adoration, she will eventually begin to see in herself the beauty you are experiencing, and she will grow richer in that beauty day by day

Einstein said there are only two ways to view the world. One is as if nothing is a miracle; the other is as if everything is. Both realities are true, and both are within your reach, but what determines your experience is your perception. Choose the former of the two perspectives and the world will bore and irritate you. Choose the latter and everyday will bring adventure. Choose the former and no one will want to be around you. Choose the latter and you will become a source of inspiration and a magnet for the best life has to offer.

Closing Remarks

Society has led us to believe that beauty has its own independent and unchanging requirements, and that we are merely passive onlookers. However, true beauty only exists by virtue of the appreciation of an observer. In other words, love is the precursor of beauty. We must therefore take an active role in nurturing and stimulating the beauty within our lady.

Beauty needs a mindful and delighted witness, otherwise it fades away. If you neglect or reject your lady, you will distance her, wound her heart and cripple her capacity for joy. You also have the power to lift her to new heights of peace, grace, and joy. Nothing you can buy with money can adorn her more splendor than the garlands of love you can provide from your heart and soul.

Pathway to Energy

Section 3

Section III dives into the invisible realm and explores the infinite expressions and dimensions of love. It reveals the hidden forces that drive our interactions and guides you through the uncharted territories of attraction, intimacy and love.

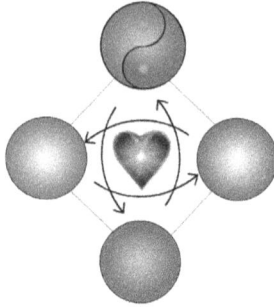

Energy
Chapter 7

«It's like a finger pointing a way to the moon. Don't concentrate on the finger, or you will miss all that heavenly glory»

~Bruce Lee

S ome men walk through this world with a fire emanating from within. Their exuberance captures you, and their energy stays with you, awakens and refreshes you. They connect with people through hidden channels, and they leave elation in their wake. Somehow, you can't pinpoint exactly what distinguishes them. Is it the way they look, the way they talk or the way they dress? No, you can't describe an external difference. To understand the difference, we must delve into the invisible world of energy.

A person who has learned to work with energy, whether consciously or not, emanates warmth and vivacity. People feel drawn to him because he has something to offer on a subtle level. To understand what separates him from other people we must investigate and study the invisible world. We must understand the nature of energy and how it drives our interactions and defines human life. If we can work well with these subtle energies, we can communicate through hidden channels, and provide our lady with the sweetest and most desirable gifts.

Introducing Energy

Every entity possesses within itself a divine energy, a life force. Science has proposed that all manifestations of matter, from the giant superstar to the tiniest subatomic particle, are essentially varying quantities and expressions of energy. All of nature operates based on the energy provided by the sun. The sun is therefore a symbol for the universal prime energy that governs all life. This founding energy is what gives life to our emotions, our love, and the innate attraction between men and women. Because it has such a huge impact on us, we are all searching for it, just as flowers face the sun as it crosses the sky.

People do many things to acquire energy, to command or attract love. Some put effort into looking good and achieving monetary success, because the admiration from their peers empowers them. Recently many are taking an interest in oriental forms of energy work, such as Thai Chi and Yoga, as it sharpens our senses, enhances our health, and gives us a taste of this all-embracing energy. Some go for drinking, over-eating, or taking drugs because it gives them an instant rush that makes them feel alive. Sadly, this harmful behavior prevents them from developing the qualities they need to sustain a true, lasting, and natural euphoria.

Many people go on a religious quest, seeking for the ultimate high of spiritual ecstasy. This is a natural foundation to fulfill the first blessing of man, but it can't stop there. What's the ultimate purpose? This universal, founding energy that sends people into transcendent consciousness has a central purpose, to help us fulfill the second blessing, the pristine union of Yin & Yang, which is the completion stage of our communion with the divine. Our experience of transcendence purifies us and elevates us so that we are better prepared to build an ideal relationship with a woman.

There are many things to learn about relating with a woman, such as what to say, how to touch, etc., and some of these ideas are expressed in this book. These techniques are meaningless, however, without an awareness of the energy currents and subtle exchanges that flow between us. Communication remains clumsy and shallow, and the deeper intimacy that we long for stays beyond our reach. This chapter, along with chapters 8 and 9, explore the principles behind spiritual energy in human relationships. If this is all new to you, you may not understand everything at first, but don't be troubled. If you make effort, you will in time be able to sense this profound yet hidden reality.

<u>Transcendent Communication</u>

Even though we live in the global era, the most interconnected era in history, we have never had more trouble connecting with each other heart-to-heart. Why is that? It is because we no longer truly pay attention to each other. We tend to practice a shallow form of communication that blinds us from intimacy.

Communication that genuinely moves us does not come through external channels such as images and words; it comes from the energy that flows within us and between us. This energy is what fills us with joy and excitement when we're around people we love.

As an illustration, picture a faucet and the water flowing through it. Some people are so concerned with making the faucet look majestic that they fail to pay attention to the water. They forget that even if the faucet is made of shining gold, it is irrelevant if the water is polluted. This is because it's not the tap we taste, but the water, and the same rings true for the interactions between people. It's not the exterior we drink and taste, but the energy that flows within our interactions. This energy is what strikes us, and when we are with the person we love, this energy is what matters.

Of course, it's important to be able to provide for a woman, please her with our gestures, and communicate with her properly, just as it is important to have a proper mechanism on a tap, so the flow of water is not too strong or too weak. All these things are important, but we must never lose touch with what truly matters: the water, the zest, the energy that moves within our interactions and relationships, the spark that makes us shiver with joy and fulfillment. What flows within is what we must cultivate.

Discovering Energy

Learning how to relate with a woman is not always a straightforward process. For this reason, it's difficult to explain through a book. A book appeals to our logic, but attraction, love and sexuality are subjects of the heart, and are not expressed primarily through reason. To understand these things, we must search our souls, our hearts and our emotions. We must dig deep to discover a subtler and richer awareness of ourselves and each other.

Improving our ability to relate with a woman requires that we learn to live with awareness of the energy within and around us. To do so, we must experience it, open our hearts to a new reality and learn to relate with the energy currents flowing all around us. Therefore, rather than explaining my realizations rationally, I will share some of my experiences with the world beyond. Hopefully you will be able to relate to my stories and begin to discover these hidden realities.

My first taste of this spiritual energy came to me when I started doing yoga. I was about eighteen at the time. I signed up for yoga because I heard it was good for my posture and that there would be many cute girls there. Those were my main motivations at the time. However, after a while, I started to experience strange sensations in my mind and body.

The first thing I noticed was getting sick. I got nauseous and dizzy after almost every practice, and when I got home, I would often throw up. My teacher explained that toxins and stress from my meridian points where released into my bloodstream causing me to get sick. I also noticed other changes. After every practice I was filled with a remarkable sense of joy and peace of mind. Because of this newfound vivacity, I started appreciating the things around me, I became more focused in my studies, and people started responding to me differently. People I had never met before would light up as I passed them on the street. This happened more than once or twice; it happened often, and at the time, I could not understand why.

One night I stayed late after class, meditating. There was a giant glass dome above me so I could see the stars shining. I felt strangely connected to them, like I was sharing their radiance. I was breathing in a feeling of contentment, and my soul was basking in the light of the stars. My mind and body connected, and just the air brushing against my face gave me bliss.

My Yoga teacher saw me meditating, and after everyone had left, she sat down in front of me. My eyes were closed, we exchanged no words, and there was no physical contact between us. Still, I could feel her presence vividly. My heart started pounding. I could feel my skin glowing, and it was as if the whole room illuminated as we connected. It was in no way a tantric or sexual experience, but our souls linked in a pure and harmonious oneness. It was as if our hearts became one. What an extraordinary experience! My body began to softly pulsate, and tears started to fall from my eyes.

I experienced a level of connection I had never felt before, and my whole being was overwhelmed with emotion. Twenty minutes, thirty minutes past and my emotions began to shift from a static pulsation to a calm soothing flow, as if an energy current were moving daintily between the two of us. I was filled with awe, but at the same time, I was utterly confused by this unprecedented experience. Finally, I stood up. I looked at her briefly and smiled. I gave her a hug and said to her, "Thank you." That was all I could say. It was all I needed to say, because we had already shared a vast ocean of inner thoughts and emotions.

***

Up until that time I had heard many things about Yoga, meditation and other eastern disciplines, but this was my first genuine experience. For the first time my mind and body opened to the energies flowing all around us, and for the first time I could truly feel another person. It filled me with uncharted inspiration. I wanted to know more about it; I had to know more about it.

I became an ardent student. I began to observe nature, music, dance, spirituality and all the things that move the heart. A new world was appearing before me. I noticed how energy moves between people as they interact, how emotions flow within their exchanges, and how these currents determine the quality of their connection.

In dance I noticed how a man can steer his woman by projecting his thoughts and emotions, and in music I learned to feel masculine and feminine vibrations harmonize with each other. In nature I discovered how the birds and animals connect. I saw how even reptiles, lacking both a neocortex, a logical center in their brain, and a paleomammalian complex, an emotional center in their brain, still were able to connect with each other. Connection and attraction, I realized, do not happen in the brain. Rather, there is a universal energy inherent to all life that causes us to respond to and affect each other, throughout the natural world.

All my life I had been passionate about how we connect as people, but at first my study was limited to techniques. I was studying how to speak more smoothly, how to listen more carefully, and how to make people laugh. These skills allowed me to engage other people, but through my new experiences with the subtle exchanges of energy, I could share in the rich inner lives of those around me. It felt like the difference between looking at a painting of the sky versus taking a day at the beach, soaking in the sun.

***

During this time, I had a hobby of going to bars to watch men trying to seduce women. I couldn't help but feel amused to see how they would boast about themselves, trying to look smooth, trying to make her laugh with their jokes, all the while talking in an artificial way and making unnatural gestures. They would tell her stories to show how exciting their lives were and buy her drinks to display their wealth. Or perhaps to get her so drunk she wouldn't notice how nervous they were. I couldn't tell for sure. They would try so hard to seduce her, yet they failed miserably, almost every time.

They failed to interest her because they did not move her heart. They were talking to her as if attraction were a mechanical process based on a checklist, as if she would say: "Okay, he has this much money, check; he has this many hobbies, check; this many friends, check; he has bought me this many drinks, check, and given me this many compliments, okay, check... Initiate attraction mode." It was certainly amusing to witness, but I couldn't help to think how inadequate this approach was.

It amused me, but it also made me thoughtful. How will the world go on if we continue like this? How can love flourish when all we think about is how to impress a woman? The truth is she is not impressed. In our insecurity and desperate efforts for validation all we do is drain her of energy.

Finally, I decided to take a break from our modern, hectic world and to immerse myself in meditation. I sought to connect with the energies around me, and after a while it was not only people I could feel. I could connect with the birds flying over my head, the animals trotting the fields, and even the trees and the flowers, and the ocean and the sun. I felt a universal prime energy in all living entities emanating love and peace.

It was such an exciting time for me. I felt connected with nature, and love filled my heart everywhere I went. I was aware that some people didn't understand me at the time, but it didn't bother me. All I knew was that I was discovering the quintessence of life that I had always been searching for.

Energy – A Living Spirit

Fast forward 3 years. In the middle of my global journey, I find myself in Texas. I just completed a 6-month exploration of the Caribbean Islands, and I decided to stop by my uncle before heading south through Mexico and eventually towards Panama.

My uncle's family is religious. A concept I found highly foreign at the time. Energy? Perhaps. Religion? Nonsense. I enjoyed two pleasant weeks with my family before heading to the airport for my flight to Cancun. I checked my email and noted down the booking number, and double-checked my bag, before catching a ride to the airport with my uncle.

Before dropping me off, my uncle told me something that has lingered in my mind to this day: "If anything goes wrong, I'll be waiting by the airport." *What a peculiar thing to say.* There was hardly any traffic at the airport, and I was about 3 hours early for my flight. What could possibly go wrong?

I went to the machine like I always do and entered my booking number. *"Invalid booking number. Please see cashier,"* lit up on the screen. *How curious.* I went to the cashier and explained the situation. She told me I was nowhere to be found in the system. I found this highly irregular since I had flown with this company more times than I could count. Because the traffic was picking up, she asked me to step aside and contact the booking company.

I accessed the airport Wi-Fi and opened my email. A new email had just appeared less than two hours prior: *"Your booking has been canceled."* *How ludicrous.* I called my booking company, and after listening to the excruciating elevator music for 45 minutes, I was finally able to square out my booking through their representative.

I went back in line to talk to the cashier. The line was considerably longer now as we approached the departure time. When it was finally my turn, a group of security guards wearing yellow reflective vests came storming into the booking area and proclaimed: "There has been a security breach; no one is allowed to board this aircraft!" I was beginning to believe the universe had an issue with me going to Mexico.

I asked the cashier about my options and she said there was another flight to Cancun later that night, but it was $387, almost four times my original ticket. I decided to explore my options with other airlines and opened my computer once more. To my great surprise, the airport Wi-Fi had stopped working.

I decided to call my uncle and explained the situation. He was still waiting right outside the airport, almost two hours later, and came right up. He explained that perhaps I was not meant to go to Mexico at this time. *Nonsense,* I thought to myself and kept persisting. I called my aunt and asked her to make the booking for me. 15 minutes later she called me back and explained that since 9/11, a new rule dictates that you can't online book an international flight less than six hours before departure. I decided to buy the overpriced ticket.

I went back to the cashier and gave her my credit card. *"Card Declined"* lit up on the screen. I never keep more than $1000 on my checking account in case of fraud, and since the other booking was still being processed, I must have been just shy. Since the airport Wi-Fi was down, I opened my mobile banking app to transfer the funds. My checking balance lit up on the front page, and I swear to God I'm not making this up: "$386." I was one dollar shy.

I accessed my savings account and prepared to transfer the funds. As I was about to press confirm, the strangest thing happened. I felt an invisible force, almost like a hand that pushed my finger to the left. I ended up pressing *"cancel"* instead of *"confirm,"* and I accidently logged out of the banking app. I tried to log back in, but suddenly, the internet on my phone had stopped working too! In this moment, I fell to my knees in frustration. I looked up at the ceiling and fiercely whispered: "Are you freaking kidding me!" I was forced to return home in defeat.

On my way back that night, I remember looking up to the stars. For the first time in my life I started to ponder: *"Perhaps this energy I have become familiar with, in fact has a personality, and perhaps it takes an interest in my affairs…"*

***

Three days later my resolve to go to Mexico had rekindled. I accessed my computer to book my ticket and started to enter my personal details. All that remained was my passport number.

I opened my bag to pull out my passport, which, to my great bewilderment, had vanished from the face of the earth. I searched frantically for two days until finally accepting it was lost. I realized I was stuck there in Texas until I could replace my passport, which according to the consulate would take at least four weeks.

My aunt told me that perhaps God had given me an opportunity to learn something. I pretended to listen to her teaching me about the ways of God, but to be perfectly honest, I wasn't particularly interested. God was too simplistic of an answer for me, but I decided to meditate and ponder what had just happened.

Every day, I sat down in the prayer room for two hours to meditate. On the fourth day something unprecedented happened. As I meditated, I suddenly felt a great fire kissing my cheeks. As I opened my eyes, all I could see was an intense bonfire. A great figure approached from my right wearing samurai-like armor. He had a long black beard and looked to be of oriental descent. I could tell this was not a physical encounter. At the same time, it felt more real than any encounter I had ever experienced before.

It felt more real because all my senses intensified. The warmth from the flames lingered in my skin, the colors of the surroundings were powerful and vibrant, and the voice of this mysterious figure resonated at the core of my heart. It appeared more concrete and substantial than the physical world, which in comparison seemed unreal, dreamlike, fuzzy and fake; like a painted veil shielding our vision from the real world.

The warrior gently brushed the ashes in the fire with his sword, before sitting down in front of me. He looked at me with kind yet thoughtful eyes emanating an ancient wisdom. His presence commanded attention and my entire being was absorbed into his energy field: a yellow glow that emanated from within him. He looked at me and spoke: "The man who does not ask, is a fool for life." Unlike physical words that enter in my ears and get processed in my brain, the words imprinted themselves deeply in my heart. It felt as though they altered my cellular structure and transformed my perceptions. After the words were uttered, the scene started to fade, the fire softened until I finally found myself back in the prayer room.

I was completely dumbfounded. What on earth just happened? I told my aunt: "I think I just saw Genghis Khan!" We searched his picture on google and I quickly discovered it wasn't him. Instead I decided to enter the phrase he told me. I had never studied Confucius at the time, I had never seen his face and I had never heard this saying before, but there he was, clearly discernible as the figure in my vision. I decided to take his counsel to heart and dedicated myself to asking questions. To question the very fabric of my belief system and to explore the ancient wisdoms of the great spiritual masters and religious founders.

Eternity

I began to investigate near-death experiences and journeys through the spiritual realm. I soon discovered a vast library of well-documented spiritual encounters like my own. I realized that human beings form a microcosm of the cosmos and along with our physical identity, we all possess an eternal spiritual identity. Corresponding to our five physical senses we have five spiritual senses that allow us to perceive the invisible world: clairvoyance, clairaudience, clairtangence, taste and smell. Just like a radio or a television that converts invisible signals into perceptible sounds and images, human beings can perceive and convert spiritual energies into meaningful messages, once we develop our spiritual faculties.

It wasn't long after I began my exploration before other encounters found me. One day while meditating in my room, trying to overcome a vexing concern in my mind, a great figure appeared in front of me: Jesus Christ. He appeared in a brilliant white light that flooded the room. His glorious presence immediately washed away the concerns of my heart and instilled my soul with a profound peace. I woke up the next day, and the major ailment I had been battling for seven years, was gone.

On another occasion, I saw Master Buddha appearing in a Baptist church. He appeared in the Maitreya Buddha form, at least 30 feet tall and shining with a soothing golden glow. He looked at me and said: "I don't know, I don't know, I don't know," as to remind me that great wisdom is given to those who ask questions.

It became clear to me that religious denominations were a fabric of human culture. Humans are experts at containing God to fit within their comfortable social sphere. "For God so loved the world that He sent his only begotten Son [for me]" they quote. Forgetting that it says: "God so loved the *world*", not "God so loved the Baptists, or the Mormons, or the Jews, or the Buddhists. God sent his Son, the great sages, the great masters, and the great philosophers, to elevate and perfect all humankind. Jesus was no Christian, Buddha was no Buddhist, and Confucius was no Confucianist. The great masters have no religious boundaries. They live and serve to the benefit of humankind.

I will not dive into the details of my spiritual experiences in this book, instead I will reserve it for a future publication. Suffice it to say that similar experiences frequently occurred during my life, and it has led me to redefine my views of the physical and spiritual world. I discovered that the energy I experienced under the glass dome with my yoga teacher, resembles the energy that religious people experience in their communion with the Divine. I understood that this energy is an all-embracing force, with an intention, personality and purpose, and that understanding this energy, was the key to succeeding in love.

***

The understanding of our two unique identities obliges us to contemplate eternity. Our physical body is merely a vessel that allows us to operate on the physical plane. It is like a cocoon that prepares us for our eternal destinies. After a short interim here on earth, we will shed our physical bodies, and enter eternity with our spiritual bodies. To prepare for the coming realm, it's essential to develop our spiritual faculties.

When we are in our mother's womb, we have little understanding of the world we are about to enter. We think this narrow and confined space is all there is. We receive all we need to sustain ourselves through the umbilical cord, so we don't ponder who might be providing it. We sense messages from the outside, and we get an intuitive understanding that there is a world beyond, and that someone there loves us, but we are likely to be content with where we are.

We have a purpose for our time in the womb, to prepare for the next realm of existence by developing our physical functions: our lungs, our legs, our hands, our brains etc. After we enter the world, it's hard to develop these functions, e.g. you can't grow an arm after you are born. Likewise, the purpose of our relatively short physical lives is to develop our spiritual faculties so to prepare ourselves for a vastly greater and less constrained realm of existence.

To develop our spiritual faculties, we must exercise our sensitivity to the world beyond, and learn to perceive invisible messages and promptings. Next, we must develop the three functions of the spirit: our heart, intellect and will. We do not breathe air in our mother's womb, so we don't strictly need lungs to survive there, but we must develop our lungs in order to thrive after we are born. In the spiritual world we don't breathe oxygen from the air either, instead we breathe in the cosmic energy of love. To prosper in the spiritual world, we must therefore develop our capacities to love, in addition to the faculties of our spirits.

We should not worry too much about physical appearances. They are temporary. Whether our spouse is short or tall, dark skinned or light skinned, has big breasts or small breasts, is of minute importance, because our body is not who we are, it's simply a temporary vehicle to be shed after a few short decades at most.

When a couple gets married, they pledge to stay together until death do them part. What a silly notion. Why would you only stay together in this limited realm of existence. Love becomes infinitely more exciting in the world beyond, provided that we have prepared ourselves accordingly. In the next world our appearances reflect our virtues. What matters is the quality of our soul, meaning our mind, heart and will. This is our inner radiance, the beauty and the light within us. These three functions are the pillars for individual perfection. A bright mind, a pure heart, and a strong will are the tools to enter Heaven, our ultimate destination.

The Invisible World

"Suppose you see a man's body stretched out on the ground. He is tangible, but he is dead; something invisible has left him, that something that once enabled him to walk, to love, to speak and to think. You can put all the food and all the treasures of the world by his side, telling him, 'there you are my friend: it's all for you. Enjoy it!' But it will not change anything; you will get no reaction." Life, the one essential element to his existence, has left him. Yet we can't see it, we can't hear it, and we can't touch it. We are all familiar with it, so we accept it to be true. We are less familiar with the invisible elements imbued in our relationships. We can't see them either, but they have defining effects.

When our relationship is void of the invisible currents that infuse life into our interactions, our connection will slowly wither. We can try to bombard it with physical treatments, but because the essential elements are gone, there is nothing we can do. We start fighting and complaining, and the tingling sensations that used to make us sing with passion for each other will eventually disappear. We can't see these invisible energies, so what can we do?

As human beings, we are experts at discrediting anything we can't see. But the reality is, the invisible world governs most of our lives. We can't see life, but it is the very element that defines our existence. A man in love has no doubts about the existence of his love. He can't see it, nor touch it, and yet he is ready to move heaven and earth because of it.

Up until a century ago we could not see micro-organisms, bacteria or parasites. We just had to accept that people got sick and died of mysterious and inexplicable causes. When Dr. Semmelweis discovered the link between child mortality and hand sanitation in the 19th century, he did so in a world without microscopes. He was ridiculed because his findings did not match conventional scientific and medical opinions, but his discoveries led to a practice that has saved millions of lives over the course of history.

Jewish people had been taught by God the practice of washing hands since ancient times, but it took millennia for technology to catch up and finally convince people. When scientific developments finally provided a way for us to see these malicious particles, a medical revolution ensued as a result. In the future, scientific instruments are likely to be further enhanced so to allow us to see all the precious elements, currently invisible, that define human life. Until that time, we must develop our sensitivity to energy and learn to use it to our advantage.

Practice your Awareness

Developing a relationship with the energies all around us is not complicated. It requires that we practice our awareness and open our spiritual senses to the invisible world. Starting with awareness, we can develop mastery over the subtle flows of energy all around us.

Experiment with your awareness. Sit down completely alone in a silent room and ask yourself, "What do I feel?" Go beyond prepackaged answers: "I feel happy" or "I feel frustrated," and pay attention to specific sensations in your body. Do you feel tension in your right shoulder, or energy moving up your leg or your spine? If that energy had a color and a shape, how would you describe it? Does it move or is it still? Does it change color, or does it remain the same? Get to know your body and mind better. You will soon gain a deeper understanding of your emotions.

Do the same while sitting out in nature. Is the feeling any different? If the birds are singing, or the wind is blowing, or the sun is shining, does it change anything? Now do the same thing around people. Do you feel stronger or weaker energy vibrations? You will soon realize that people do emanate energy, and you can feel it through careful attention.

Familiarize yourself with the energy currents transmitted between people. Notice if some people make your heart pump faster, and if others make you nervous and sweat. Now ask yourself, "How do other people perceive me?" and, "What type of energy currents am I projecting?" Practice your ability to enhance your energy projections by making them more vibrant and luminous. Our aura reflects the inner contents of our souls, and is colored by our virtues, habits and personalities. To brighten and intensify our auras, we must first work on our character traits, but we can add further flavor and purity by our intentions and focus. This all starts with awareness.

Emotions

Emotions are energies in motion. Perhaps that's why they are called "E-motions." Whenever you feel an emotion, be it love, happiness, sadness, anger, joy or excitement, it is because energy is moving in your body. The best way to identify and develop mastery over energy is therefore to work with your emotions. This is an enduring theme throughout this book.

Our emotions affect much more than the way we feel. They affect our thoughts, words, and actions. They also affect the people around us. If you allow negative energy to fill your heart, then it will influence your aura, and affect the way others perceive you. If, on the other hand, you can use your willpower and awareness to transform your emotions into positive vibrations, then they can inspire and bring life to others.

Your emotions can be your greatest blessing or your greatest affliction. It all depends on how you treat them. Many people, due to their lack of awareness of the impact of their emotions, develop serious problems. But if you master your emotions, you can use them to do marvelous works. Just like different qualities of microorganisms exists, that either heal us or make us sick, there are different qualities of energy that rejuvenate us or break us down. To ensure that the energy we project is lifegiving, we must nourish our spirits with the right type of elements, (more on this in Chapter 12).

Be vigilant with your emotions and thoughts. Be careful with the thoughts and emotions you entertain and the activities you engage in. The qualities of the activities and elements you entertain, will directly affect the type of energy currents you transmit to others. Luminous energy projections are obtained by luminous thoughts and emotions, so monitor yourself, educate yourself, and control the environment of your inner world. Live a life free from shadows and engage with lifegiving media and activities. You will soon see your energy currents, and thus the quality of your life and relationships, transformed.

Learning to work with energy is in many ways synonymous with learning to work with your emotions and your thoughts. The thoughts and emotions we entertain become the energy we project to others. They also influence the types of invisible particles we attract and thus affect our quality of life. Rather than making an external effort in your pursuit towards a greater love life, start tapping into the unseen qualities that infuse your interactions with vitality, and lend life to your smallest gestures. Learn to understand and master the underlying currents of energy that saturate our existence. The awareness and mastery of this energy will enable you to communicate on subtle levels and will demystify the unseen essence of human relationships.

Closing Thoughts

At the dawn of my journey I set out to learn about women, but what I discovered was far more interesting. As stated in the introduction, it felt as if I asked for a cup of water but was launched into the Pacific Ocean. I discovered it was easy to learn how to talk to a woman, how to flirt, how to give her comfort and how to play with her. It was much more difficult to learn how to work with energy, yet this was what made all the difference. It's difficult because most of us lack a concept of energy. We think that belief in Chi, energy flow, and the spiritual world, is a quaint and discredited superstition ascribed to ancient religious cults or Buddhist temples. But what I realized is that this life force is well-documented and widely affirmed, and it's also accessible to experience for ourselves.

Various religious and philosophical institutions describe this force in complimentary yet conflicting ways. It seems they have all touched a different part of a proverbial elephant. To see the whole elephant, we must study the vast knowledge handed down through various expressions over the centuries and combine it with our own personal perceptions and experiences. Once we begin to explore, this reality will gradually unfold before us.

By learning to work with energy we can taste the true quintessence hidden throughout the natural world. We can develop our internal attributes so that the energy we emit is warm and caring, rather than tiresome. Also, by learning to communicate through energies and emotions, we are no longer limited to our words and gestures only, or relegated to flaunting our status symbols, as many feel the need to do. Our presence will communicate a world of riches.

Evolving in our spiritual abilities allows us to become truly intimate with our sweetheart and enables us to provide for her the love and life she desperately needs and deserves from us. Part of this evolution and self-mastery depends on our knowledge of the masculine/feminine polarity inherent in the life force we are studying. In the following chapter we will investigate the principles behind attraction, and unravel the mysteries of Yin & Yang, the feminine and masculine dynamic.

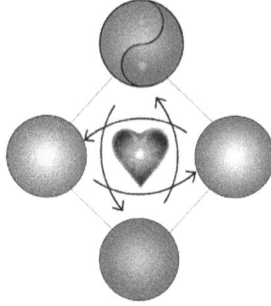

Yin & Yang

Chapter 8

«Countless words count less than the silent balance between Yin & Yang»

~Lao Tzu

I wrote this book, and you are reading this book, all because of the inescapable power of the feminine mystique. No matter how great we are, we can never escape the need for a woman's touch. We are dominated by this need because it stems from the fundamental principle by which we were created. How do we understand this ancient and all-consuming mystery that binds us into an inescapable bond with the feminine? How do we enhance it, and how do we use it to elevate our relationships? Let's dive into this primordial dance between the feminine and masculine principles, let's look at the core substance defining the attraction between Yin & Yang, and let's discover how to kindle the fire in our beloved's yearning heart.

In its simplicity, nature reveals to us the essence of attraction. The positive pole of a magnet attracts the negative pole because this attraction is inherent. The fact that a man needs a woman, and a woman needs a man is an absolute, undeniable reality. The very existence of our race depends on it. The complementary opposites of masculine and feminine, positive and negative, are ever-present throughout nature. The existence of all matter and all life depends on this dynamic.

In this chapter, we will discover the unique value of each gender and learn to stimulate their complementary qualities. We will look at the powerful interplay of Yin & Yang, and finally, we will learn to discover and claim our manhood. Through this process we will stimulate our girl's ability to embrace her sweet femininity and establish a lasting and vibrant magnetism between us.

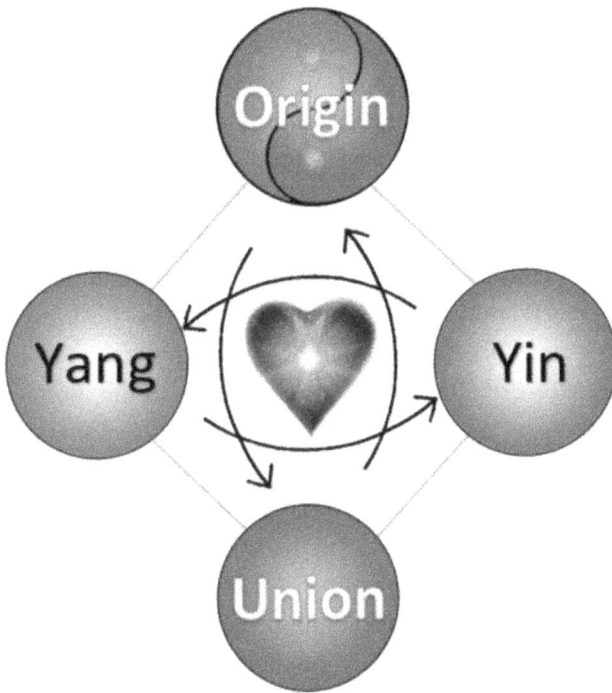

The Four-Position Foundation

What is attraction? Is it a simple phenomenon that occurs at nightclubs after enough tequila shots? Is it something that emerges after enough jewelry has been bought, enough doors have been opened and enough compliments have been given? The answer is indeed far more exhilarating. The bond between Yin & Yang is part of a cosmic principle that govern all interactions in our known universe, from the interplay of the electron and the proton to the motions of the galaxies. The knowledge of this principle is the key to enliven the spark in our relationships.

The four-position foundation illustrates the relationship between the Origin (Taiji), Yin and Yang, and their Union. Let us try to understand each station individually, starting with the Origin. Love and life flow from an original source. This is demonstrated by the law of entropy, exemplified by our ever-expanding universe and symbolized by the dynamic interplay between the sun and the earth. The earth doesn't generate the energy required to sustain the interactions on our planet. All energy is received from the sun, which is then transfigured into beautiful expressions through the magnetic interactions on earth. This source is known by many names. Which religious or philosophical faculty we prescribe to is irrelevant. What matters is we seek to connect with the original source of love and life, drink and savor its nectar, and allow it to revitalize our spirits and minds.

The next stations in the four-position foundation is Yang and Yin, the subject and the object, the masculine and the feminine. It doesn't require much observation to realize that all interactions in our universe involve the principles of Yin & Yang. The subatomic universe is governed by the interactions of the proton and the electron, the atomic universe is governed by anions and cations. Molecules are also bonded and formed through negative and positive forces and thus shape our material universe. In the plant kingdom, stamen and pistil govern the process and creation of life. In the animal kingdom there is male and female, and in the human kingdom there is man and woman. All entities in the known universe manifest specific masculine and feminine attributes. Whether this polarity is expressed as negative-positive, internal-external, hot-cold, north-south, or masculine-feminine, the inescapable truth is that that all things possess the dual characteristics of Yin & Yang. These principles are all-embracing and necessary to sustain love and life.

We might be tempted to believe in a world of sameness, where men and women are indistinguishable. But this contradicts the fundamental principles for which our universe is founded. If all protons became electrons, the material universe would cease to exist. Likewise, if all men became women, life would end. Obviously because no more children would be born, but also because the savory juices generated from our interactions would slowly fade. To rekindle the fire in our lives and relationships, we must reclaim our manhood and offer our lady the freedom to be truly feminine. This is what much of this chapter is dedicated to.

The last station of the four-position foundation is the Union. The original source is divided into Yin and Yang, and when these principles inevitably rejoin, a union and a result is formed, unique from the source. When the sunbeam penetrates the soil, life begins to grow, flowers begin to bloom, birds begin to sing, and the rivers begin to flow. When a man and a woman come together, euphoria is released, and a child is formed, unique and magnificent. When our mind and body, another image of Yin & Yang, is united, creative ideas begin to flow, and new ideas, artistries and inventions are born.

Each time the four-position foundation is fulfilled, new and brilliant expressions of beauty, love and creativity are conceived. These expressions are both unique and superior to the principles from which they were formed. From the four-position foundation, our universe is sustained and continues to evolve. Because the energy from the source is inexhaustible, and because the dynamic interaction between Yin and Yang continues to breed new exciting unions, the universe continues to grow and continues to offer new and exhilarating expressions of joy and beauty.

Yin & Yang

To gain a deeper understanding of the masculine and the feminine, and to learn how to interact with our beloved, we should study the source of Yin & Yang interactions. The living book of nature contains the secret and the original substance of the masculine and feminine communion.

Study the ocean, a perfect symbol of the feminine; gentle, constant, vast and beautiful. At the same time, it's powerful, vital and fierce. It holds abundant life and provides nourishment for all within and many on land. The ocean's embrace covers most of the earth. If we look to the mountains - strong, grounded, lofty, majestic – an expression of the singular glory of masculine energy is revealed. The root of the mountain, the tectonic plates, lies underneath as bedrock and provides the foundation on which the ocean rests. The ocean is concave, and the mountain is convex, the ocean is fluid and all-embracing, and the mountain is firm and penetrating.

If you look at the way the ocean and the mountain interact, you will see masculine/feminine interplay. The ocean softly strokes the mountain with gentle waves, or it strikes with fiery passion. Regardless, the mountain stands firm as if to say, "I am here, and I will not move. I will support you no matter what." There are so many ways that nature provides us with insight into the quintessential natures of men and women.

If you go to the park or into the forest, you will see myriad forms of life and love. Plants reveal the principles of masculine and feminine working together to produce life. A seed germinates in the soil, and over time, it springs forth into a beautiful flower. The seed is masculine; it contains the DNA, the blueprint which provides the direction and purpose for its development. The soil is feminine, the "Mother Earth," and she provides for the seed a safe and nurturing environment. The seed needs additional masculine and feminine elements from its environment as well. Masculine sunlight emanates from above, penetrating the soil with its rays and provides energy and warmth for the seed. Feminine water flows from the earth below and nourishes the body of the plant.

The most endearing and somewhat astonishing arena for nature's expression of the masculine/feminine dynamic can be found in the study of various mating rituals and the care for the newly born. The male bird calls out to his female counterpart, courting her with a special song. The female resists at first but is eventually drawn to his inescapable and persistent masculine pull. At last, she responds, the mating dance commences, and chicks are born. The male peacock dramatically woos his mate by displaying his colorful appendage. The extensive and lovely mating dances of water birds and bowerbirds also provide a lovely surprise to your most casual observer.

The salmon run is a fascinating display of the struggle for mating privilege. The male salmon gives his life to the weeks long treacherous trail to the mating ground. He fights for his life through the impossible force of the river steps and the alluring dangers of bear attacks, all to reach the mating grounds. Here he has now gained the right to partake in the glorious mating dance, before he satisfyingly dies from exhaustion, knowing he has fulfilled the purpose for his life. Taking a moment to observe the noble seasonal rituals of various members of the animal kingdom engaged in mating and bringing new life into this world leaves us in awe of nature's stunning artwork. It also helps us connect with the primordial source of Yin & Yang interactions.

No book can fully explain the nature of Yin & Yang, because it is not a subject grasped fully by our intellect. We can't know the taste of honey without eating it, and we can't know the color of the sky except by seeing it. Understanding masculine and feminine energy is a matter of the heart, and it must be experienced. Your textbook is wide open and all around you; everything you need to know is inscribed in the living book of nature. If you study nature closely, vivid realizations will come to you. Seek therefore to experience the masculine and the feminine in its purest form and engrave this ancient wisdom into your heart and soul. This is the essential wisdom that allows you to reach new heights in your romantic relationship.

Man & Woman

Who is more valuable? Man or woman? Most people would agree that this is an absurd question, because one without the other, just like the electron without the proton, has no substantial value. Only in their union can they attain their potentials.

They are equal, certainly, but equality doesn't mean sameness. We must separate the idea of value from the idea of position. Each gender has supreme value, but their roles are different. We must expand our understanding of value to include both feminine and masculine traits and recognize that the value of each is realized through their union.

A man is superior to a woman in some areas and a woman is superior to a man in other areas. It's well-known that men can run faster, lift heavier and jump higher. Men are more suited to make certain strategic decisions, because they can typically keep multiple variables and possible scenarios in mind and carry these to their logical conclusions. For this reason, men are better at tactics, and will most likely beat a woman in chess. Men also excel at visualizing blueprints and three-dimensional images, so they are good at designing and building, as well as reading maps. A man's peripheral vision is narrower than a woman's. He is therefore less able to catch peripheral details, but better able to see at a distance. Furthermore, men are superior in certain expressions of the will. Once a man has set his objective, he's able to maintain his focus through seemingly impossible hardships to achieve his purpose. This makes him an ideal provider.

In what realms are the woman superior to the man? Women are as different from men as the Earth is different from the Sun. Women have distinct brain function patterns. They have the ability to consider myriads of dissimilar demands and circumstances and can use a holistic approach when solving problems. Where men try to break through the opponent's defenses, women can discover mutually beneficial solutions. Through their nurturing instinct, they cultivate patience and endurance, and because of the depth of their emotions, they develop their famous intuition, which makes them excel with human relationships. Most importantly, they're soft and smell nice, and if not for them, all refrigerators would have nothing but Chinese take-out and twinkies!

According to the book of Genesis, woman is the final creation, the omega. It can be said that she is the crowning glory and fulfillment of the purpose of the universe. If man is bone, woman is flesh. If man is the Sun, she is the Moon and the Earth. If man is Truth, she is Love. In pursuing a world of peace, I believe women will be the future global benefactors. Men typically want to be heroes and go all out to try to change the world through brute force. Women usually have a deeper sense of the true agents of change inherent in building relationships. Their patience and understanding of conflict resolution and of human relationships make them better suited than men to facilitate peace.

Gandhi and Dr. King showed us that the force of the human conscience and the power of compassion are our greatest assets, and that the best way to destroy an enemy is to make of him a friend. We are entering the era of women; we need the logic of love in order to build our new world and will therefore do well to empower women and seek out their wisdom.

Masculine & Feminine

When we understand the absoluteness of the masculine and the feminine, we also understand the necessity of cultivating them each individually. Unfortunately, our society follows a different trend. In the twentieth century the women's liberation movement moved society forward, ensuring that women gained the right to vote and to compete in the workforce, in the government, and in every area of society. Unfortunately, the value of the role that women play within the family has become denigrated.

114

Modern women pursue personal independence, excellence in sports, financial success and freedom, and even sexual conquests. Women are encouraged to take charge and be initiators. Boys, on the other hand, should restrain themselves. They are forbidden from expressing virility in school and are required to sit still and "be good." Boys and men are to be emotionally sensitive, to cry freely, and even whine. If men demonstrate the strength that women are encouraged to, then society accuse them of misogyny. As a result, women have become masculine and men are emasculated. What we wanted was equality, but what we got is bland homogeny. Equality would mean that the two distinct genders have an absolute unique value. Instead we have idealized sameness and have demonized the natural expression of gender differences.

Of course, given the androgyny played out in modern relationships, many men proclaim, "There is no fire between me and my lady." And women are in tears asking, "Where are all the real men?" The truth is they are extinguished through false cultural convictions. The problems lie in our lack of polarity. We fail to draw out what's unique and best in each other. Instead of trying to please a woman by being one of her girlfriends, men should cultivate their masculinity. Women should not blame men either. They have the power to draw out a man's masculinity by approaching him with tenderness, affection and with their natural and original feminine beauty. If we empower each other in this way, then the fire will surely rekindle.

Our society doesn't teach men what it means to be men, and it doesn't teach women to embrace their femininity. Ideally, parents should mentor their sons and daughters, and help them mature into their respective roles. Children also need to see their fathers and mothers passionately embrace each other, harmonizing the opposite but complementary parts that each gender plays. We must cherish each other and celebrate that we are different, wonderfully different. Our ability to get along can't depend on pretending that we are identical. If we continue to fall for this ruse, we will never enjoy passion as couples.

Our job as men is to embrace our masculine nature. It is the greatest gift we can offer to a woman and to the world. We must ignore some of the recently fabricated rules and pursue a higher ideal: the ideal of masculine and feminine harmony, a reflection of the original cosmic principle.

Masculine Edge

What does it mean to be a man? Does it mean to be strong and fierce, to strut around in an oil-stained muscle shirt, fixing motorbikes? Or how about this, to be refined and confident, to sport a three-piece suit whenever we walk out the door, and to spend the day ordering people around? No, masculinity is not about external trappings. True masculinity has to do with our maturity and sense of responsibility. It's related to our inner strength, to having the self-awareness and confidence to take care of ourselves and the people we love.

It's our mission as men to cultivate our masculine edge, to become protectors, lovers and providers. Our qualities draw out our lover's tender beauty. We provide for her a sanctuary, and a place to blossom. Our confidence, courage, and our deep longing for her has the power to instill her with sacred joys. Even so, many men are unable to make a woman shine because they have lost the masculine edge that defines them as men.

Previous generations didn't have this problem because boys would take after their fathers. A father would teach his son how to make a fire, how to wield an ax, how to farm, and how to treat his lady. From his father, a boy learned to be a man; he did not need further education. Sadly, many boys today grow up without a father figure. For this reason, they grow up without a clue about how to be a man, or how to relate with a woman.

In addition to the failure of fathers to raise their sons, a second common void in the lives of young men is the lack of a rite of passage: a ritual to prove their manhood. Since there's no way to show that they have left childhood behind, and since immature behavior is now acceptable, some boys never make it past adolescence. As a result, women have no choice but to partner with immature men. Because he's irresponsible and immature, a woman can't afford to defer to his judgment or to rely on his promises. She can't fully adopt a feminine role because he's not strong enough to support her.

To regain our masculine strength, we must restore and reclaim these two lost elements. We must delve into the world of men and discover what true masculinity entails, and we must endure a rite of passage to claim our manhood.

Masculine Stimulation

We are part of a generation raised by women. Because of divorce and abandonment, many fathers live apart from their families. Many of those who live with their wives and children are still nearly absent, due to long hours at work. When they finally come home, they are too tired to enjoy time with their sons. Also, from kindergarten through high school, most teachers are women. Young boys are thus raised by women and taught to follow feminine role models and values.

Many young boys are taught from childhood to follow the examples set by the girls. If they play tough or make noise, they're told to stop, to play "nicely," in other words, quietly, "like the girls." The boys are thereby taught to submit to women, to see feminine demeanor as the only civilized choice, and to hold up feminine behavior as ideal. When they grow up, they are unable to stand solid, as head of their households, and will instead wait patiently and quietly, for their lady to give them directions and tell them what do to. They become submissive and receptive, and they expect their lady to be a giver and initiator.

Because of our socialization this pattern may feel natural, but the truth is, this destroys the hope for a harmonious relationship; it is deadly to us as individuals and terminal for the joy in a household. It makes women wonder why their men are so void of passion, and it makes men wonder why their relationship is so dry and boring. To cure this dreadful reality, we must reclaim our manhood and express our masculine edge. Then we will find that our beloved breathes a sigh of relief and begins to see us with a new level of respect and adoration.

To reclaim our manhood, we must make effort. The most crucial elements of claiming our masculinity has to do with developing our characters. We must develop emotional discipline, dignity, a vision and a strategy in life, as well as the ability to sacrifice ourselves in the service of those we love. These topics have been extensively covered so far in the book because they are the framework for our masculine edge. Beyond strengthening our characters, a way to further build our masculinity is to seek out masculine stimulation. Here are a few places to begin:

1. Spend Time with Honorable Men

Spend time with men you respect. Solid friendships with honorable men draw out your masculinity. Choose to surround yourself with men dedicated to enhancing their masculinity and who deeply treasure their spouses (avoid "women-haters.") Go fishing, take a hike in the mountains, go hunting or watch a football game. Share your heart with your friends. Be honest and inspire each other to stand as responsible, mature, strong men in relationship to other people, to your children, and to the women of your lives. Support each other, confide in each other, and push each other to a higher standard. Through this time with your friends, you will gain a new sense of strength and centeredness. When you return to your girl, she will notice your masculine exuberance. You will have reestablished polarity in your love-life, and thus discover a newfound fondness for each other.

2. Connect with Your Father.

Many men have a sour relationship with their fathers. As discussed, problems in this relationship often create an inability to bond with other men and a lack of masculine identity. It is therefore essential to establish a solid relationship with your father. If your father is not alive, reevaluate your past, try to understand the pain he went through, and forgive him for his mistakes. If he is still alive, seek to connect with him. Try to understand his heart and the love he has for you. Most likely there are many things he has wanted to tell you, but never could.

The lack of masculine edge is often a hereditary problem, and if you can forgive your father for his mistakes, you can start to rebuild the masculine strength in your family. Connecting with your father, and seeking to understand his perspective, will often lead to resolved inner conflicts and confusions about your identity, and give you shoulders to stand upon when embracing your masculine edge. Reaching out to your father may not be easy for you, but if you overcome your hesitation, you will take a solid step toward healing one of the most important relationships in your life.

3. Indulge in Masculine Recreation

Go out in the woods, wield your ax, go hunting, get your hands dirty, work on your car, go to the gym and pump iron. Go bungy jumping, shark diving, or face your fear. Or even simpler, watch an action movie or go to a NASCAR rally or a football game. All these stereotypically masculine activities get your testosterone boiling, and sure enough, you begin to feel like a man.

When you put yourself in a situation that calls you to assert your manhood, you begin to feel your masculinity bubbling inside. Most of the time we are so captive to unspoken social demands that we become androgynous and unassertive. But when we go for the masculine in our environment and in ourselves, we break from these bizarre social requirements, and we discover the man repressed but alive deep within us. Your girl will notice him too, trust me.

The Rite of Passage

Throughout history men have participated in rites of passage. In primitive tribes, young boys were sent into the wilderness without food or water, to claim their manhood. They must have been frightened in the face of danger and privation, but they found their courage in surviving their ordeal and took their places beside their fathers. They discovered that they could make it on their own in the darkest places, and through this experience, they unleashed the masculine power latent within them.

Today we are robbed from such a ritual. It's up to the individual to find his strength, and many men never do. The rite of passage ensured that a young man was worthy of the trust of other men and that he could raise and protect a family. The women also knew they could trust his maturity and masculinity. They were comfortable following such a man to the ends of the earth, because they could trust his ability to care for them. All men should go through some type of rite of passage before they take a partner and start raising a family. They should be given the opportunity to endure hardship and to claim their manhood, and they should be given education and instruction on what it means to be a man and how to take care of a family. They should learn to treasure their manhood and be proud of their unique identities.

Since society no longer provides such a rite, we must create one ourselves. The actual content of our passage is individual. I'd like to assure you that you don't have to run into the wilderness with a Tarzan loincloth and chase wild panthers but allow your heart to guide you and choose a journey meaningful to you. You might travel around the world or pursue a long-cherished dream. You may choose to go down a career path you never dared to try, or take up martial arts, or mountain climbing, or face a deeply rooted fear. Perhaps you would choose a spiritual path and seek the divine through meditation and prayer. Your passion might drive you to write a book or establish a business or a non-profit organization. It's your decision. Search your heart for what is lacking in your life, and you will find it. All these choices are valuable avenues to reach a level of self- trust and maturity.

My Rite of Passage

When I was nineteen, I discovered that something was missing in my life. I was an engineering student at the time, attending one of the top universities in Europe. I was following what I believed to be my best option, but I soon realized my path was not truly my own. All I did was follow the path that society had laid out before me. I had no foundation to understand my true calling, because I had no experience outside of the narrowly defined set of expectations imposed by my society.

I discovered I was not a man. Who was I to take care of a lady and raise a child? I was barely in control of my own life. A light went on for me one day, and I realized I had to get out of my bubble and experience the world. I needed to know what was out there, and what it meant to be a man.

One day I walked up to my professor in the middle of class and told him that I was planning to leave the university. I asked if I could say a few words to the assembly of about five hundred students. My exact words to my peers were something like, "All my life I have followed what I believed to be right, but now I realize that I have no foundation to know what is right. I want to understand and immerse myself in true passion. I hope that your motivation for studying engineering is deeply rooted in your hearts, and I wish you all the best. I hope I will see you again someday." I nodded to a few friends as I left the auditorium, and the next day I was on a one-way flight to Spain.

My destination was a small town on the south coast. I chose it because I knew it would be deserted for the winter, and I lived alone in an apartment by the sea. I kept to myself because I needed solitude and time to think through my many questions. It must have been hard for my family that I didn't call home much. I was on an inner journey, searching for truth, and I couldn't allow myself to be distracted. After three months in deep contemplation, I gained clarity. I didn't yet know my path in life, but I knew it would be different. I decided I had much more to investigate.

I returned to Oslo, the capital of Norway, so I could make money for my next journey. After 5 months of working as a salesman, I bought a world map and a dart, and I decided to leave my fate in the hands of higher powers. I threw the dart blindly and it landed in the Caribbean Sea, just outside of Jamaica. I bought a one-way ticket and left with nothing more than a four-point-five kilo backpack. I didn't know when I would return, only that it would not be until I had found what I was looking for.

I visited all the major islands in the Caribbean, staying off the tourist routes so I could get to know the locals. My mind expanded in ways I could never have imagined. I got to know the true meaning of poverty. Many nights I slept under the stars and relied only on bananas and coconuts to satisfy my hunger. I lost my credit card in Cuba, so I had to learn the language very quickly. Even though I had no money, I felt like I couldn't just stop traveling, so I rode cross-country in big trucks, together with almost two hundred other people. It was so hot, and the air was so terrible that I almost fainted several times. I kept hitching these rides for five weeks, until I finally got my new credit card. I learned a lot about my personal boundaries at that time.

When I walked through the streets, I saw people in need, forced to sell their bodies in order to feed their families. People literally lived in boxes, struggling to survive starvation. It made me think of all the abundance that I had overlooked in my country. Even though I saw so much suffering, I also discovered joy. Wherever I went, people were celebrating life. In the villages of Jamaica, I saw celebrations on almost every street corner, people playing drums and children dancing to the rhythms. It made me laugh and cry with joy. I learned from them that life itself is a reason to celebrate, and no matter the hardships, we must always appreciate the things we have.

With this experience behind me, I set my course to the United States. I wanted to see the center of the known world up close. Unfortunately, I was depressed by what I saw. My first destination was Las Vegas. Everything was so glamorous and extravagant, but under the facade there was much suffering. I witnessed material obsession, people always looking for something bigger, better, faster, stronger. I got the feeling that people's souls were consumed by their desires. I also witnessed prostitution and drug abuse, and so many people whose only purpose seemed to be their own immediate pleasure. The impressive buildings soon lost any appeal to me.

I realized from these experiences that joy does not come from what we have externally, but rather, from the abundance in our hearts. I finally came face to face with the part of myself that I had neglected, my spirituality. I decided to immerse myself in the works of the great masters; I studied teachings from all the major religions, and I researched all the mysteries of the human heart. I became utterly intrigued. A new world was opening before me, and I knew I had to fully explore it at its source. I set my course towards Asia.

I spent two months living in a spiritual training center in the mountains of South Korea. My journey so far had given me many challenges, but this was beyond any doubt the hardest time in my life. We slept on the floor, sometimes for as little as four hours a night, and the food was very simple. But that wasn't what made my stay difficult. I had become used to far worse conditions. What was hard for me was that I felt compelled to let go of many of my beliefs about life. Every day I listened to the teachings of great spiritual masters and spent time alone in the mountains. From five in the morning to eleven at night, I was completely absorbed in contemplation and meditation. I realized that many of my old views just didn't fit with the reality confronting me in this unfamiliar part of the world.

This mountaintop experience transformed my character. My values and priorities changed, and I began to see my life according to a broader perspective. I understood that life only has meaning if you contribute to other people. The only true value of life is measured by your love for others.

It took me two years to complete my rite of passage, but I finally returned home. I experienced more during this time than I thought I ever would in a lifetime, and my discoveries surprised me and changed me in ways I can't even put into words. I gained a new direction in life, and I finally felt confident calling myself a man.

There were many things I needed to understand, and perhaps for this reason my journey was rather extreme. Your journey does not have to take you far and wide, but it is vital that it takes you out of your comfort zone and gives you the chance to earn the self-respect and self-confidence that you associate with manhood. What matters is that you follow your intuition about what is missing in your life. Through your adventure you will discover a whole new world. I promise you that the insights you receive will be far more profound than any book or seminar can ever reveal to you, and I promise you they will take you far beyond the scope of your original questions. So set sail and enjoy the breeze on your face.

Closing Remarks

Women, like our universe, are at once mysterious and simple. The vast and magical mysteries of Yin stand as our counterpart within the greater majesty of this simply elegant, many-faceted universe. They are completely unique and at the same time an inherent part of who we are. We can never become a mature man, we can never fulfill our true masculinity, until we are one with our beloved. She is essential to our manhood, just as the earth is essential to the tree, and as the concept of up is necessary to understand the notion of down.

We have celebrated her unique attributes and come to appreciate the grandeur dignity inherent to our own masculinity. We have explored the methods and pathways that enable us to construct the bedrock of our own masculinity, so to be able to bring the riches of the masculine spirit to a committed relationship. Now, let's discover the qualities inherent in an ideal union. Let's explore the qualities and the wisdom of the perfect lover.

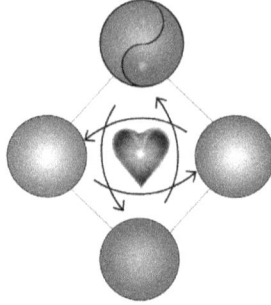

The Perfect Lover

Chapter 9

«True love is born from understanding»

~Gautama Buddha (Apocryphal)

T he world is full of opportunities. We can be anywhere on the surface of the earth in a matter of hours. We can pursue any career, any idea, any amusement, and we can learn about anything at the touch of a button. But in this frenzy of possibilities, many of us are confused and lonely. It's as if our inner eye has no idea of which way is up, or as if our eyes can't work together so we see double all the time. The remedy for this confusion is simple, even if it's not that obvious or easy to accomplish. Peace of mind comes to us when we lay aside our miscellaneous aspirations and make love our central priority. As we savor and cultivate the quality of love within our relationship, we will find meaning in the humblest of routines. Whereas before our challenges seemed overwhelming, we now have confidence to face them.

The power of true love smooths over conflicts and makes burdens seem light. It makes our relationships rich with the various colors and textures of emotion, and glorious in its power to uplift and inspire us. When a man and a woman perfect their love, they have attained their ultimate purpose. This love has a ripple effect that touches the globe as well as our household.

This chapter is about becoming perfect lovers. Our failure in love comes in large from a lack of understanding. When we understand love, and practice it, then we can offer our beloved the most sought-after, long-cherished elixir of eternal life: true love in its pristine form and substance.

Love & Beauty

The deepest dream of a woman is the blessed assurance stemming from an eternal oneness with her devoted lover. She will sacrifice everything she has, everything she is, and everything she will ever be to know this bliss. The reason, however, that many men fail in their relationships is that they do not know what love really means. This fundamental ignorance tears relationships apart.

The English language is desolate in its expression for love; the word encapsulates innumerable categories of affection. To describe our love for our dog, our love for our country, our love for ice-cream and our love for our woman with the same word, seems hopelessly misleading. We are not born with the ability to love a woman. A baby responds to his mother's love with the love of an infant, which over time blossoms into the love children have for their parents. This love develops still more through the relationships he shares with his siblings and friends, until he is at last mature enough to appreciate, nourish and support a partner. The ability to nurture a person's soul requires practice and maturity. Of course, it makes a woman happy if you like the shape of her body or the way she cooks, but this is not true love. For her to feel truly fulfilled, you must nourish her soul. This ability does not simply come to you; it is developed through consistent, concentrated effort over time.

It's odd that people recognize the effort and education needed to succeed in a career but expect true love to be as easy as eating cake. Of course, it's easy to appreciate the beauty of a woman you meet by chance in passing. But the ability to genuinely care for another person, to build strong understanding and trust, and to deepen that union through all life's challenges, requires ardent study and practice.

A man must take initiative to be successful in his relationship with his beloved. She depends on him to take this step, and if he waits for his lady to initiate, he will fail to realize the true magic inherent in their union.

His ability to see the beauty, purity, charm, and greatness in his partner determines how these qualities develop within her. Love and beauty are eternally connected. A woman who is loved becomes beautiful, just like a flower that is cared for blooms longer, and a dog that is loved has a shinier coat. Wherever there is beauty, there is love, and wherever there is love, there is beauty.

As investigated through the four-position foundation diagram from Chapter 8, for love to flow there must be an initiating partner giving affection and a receptive partner returning beauty. Notice, I did not say the reverse. Beauty is actualized in response to love, not the other way around. To illustrate the dynamic of subject and object, picture a performer relating to his audience. A performer is meaningless without an audience, and an audience is meaningless without a performer. Put a virtuoso on a deserted island, and he will never experience joy. The artist and audience, subject and object, lover and beloved, only experience joy in harmony; they are inseparable and absolutely dependent of each other.

Nature is organized according to cosmic principles. The masculine principle initiates and the feminine principle responds. Through this circulative dynamic, nature's splendid interactions unfold. Likewise, in an ideal relationship between man and woman, the man is the initiating partner, or subject, and the woman is the receptive partner, or object. It's the man's job to initiate love. His role is to discover her true inner beauty and to draw it out from its inner dwelling place. If he can focus his loving attention on her, she will radiate beauty back to him. Perhaps you have noticed that happily married women become stunningly attractive? Their interplay with their partner yields joy and makes them shine. We can even say that this interplay is at the heart of the purpose of life. It generates the inexhaustible force of true love, which is the secret to eternal life.

Of course, there are times in a healthy relationship when your beloved will initiate love. She will feel free to reach out to you and pull you with her feminine mystique. Sometimes she will take on a motherly role in caring for you. This makes a relationship deeper and richer. When it comes to the relationship overall however, a man should be in the position to initiate, to draw his darling to himself and scoop her into his arms with vivacity and affection.

Men like a challenge and the pursuit of their goals. We enjoy the chase, the climb, the hunt. When a woman keeps mystery about herself and keeps herself just out of reach, it's tantalizing! When she has captured your full attention, and knows that you are entirely hers, she will gradually allow you to come near, turn to you, and open herself to you.

A mature woman has within her soul a furnace and a palace of love. Within her palace you can be refreshed by bathing in her beauty and get lost in the vast ocean made from her euphoric affection. But for this sacred space to come into existence, you must really see her, invest your heart in your relationship, and pursue her again and again. If you expect her to pursue you while you take on a passive role, then the tension and power of the pursuit evaporates. You become the feminine, she becomes the masculine, and the power of polarity fades away.

If you want lightning and thunder, then you need certain atmospheric conditions. A high-pressure front meets a low-pressure front, hot and cold currents collide, and boom! This tension between the masculine and feminine natures keeps love and life exciting forever.

I can imagine that you know some women will bristle at the idea that a man plays the subjective role. Women have been oppressed throughout history and are no longer able to trust in men's leadership. This reality compels women to resist their own feminine nature. Some women have been educated that there is no value or honor in the feminine role. To mend the historic injustice suffered by women, you must prove to her your valor and worthiness of trust. Develop the strength and flexibility to consider the views of those in your care. It's critical to your relationship that you cherish your beloved's thoughts and feelings. She will discover things that escape you and understand things that you are not aware of. If you are mature and confident in yourself, able to hear her voice and take her views into consideration, and if you treat her with love and understanding, she will come to respect your natural authority and be proud to stand by your side, in a supportive and empowering role.

Philautia - Self-Love

"All friendly feelings for others are an extension of a man's feelings for himself."
~Aristoteles

Loving a lady well means being able to see her, to understand her, to protect her and to lead her. The art of loving in this way demands that we develop our capacity for love in all contexts, in all relationships, with people and with nature. The place to start, is with the man in the mirror.

Jesus said that the second most important of all of God's 613 Mosaic laws is to "love your neighbor as you love yourself." He referred to the certainty that you must love yourself in order to love others. When your cup is already overflowing, you don't need to beg for water, you can freely give, with no strings attached.

When you dislike yourself, on the other hand, your insecurity and negative thought patterns cloud your vision of the world. You become blinded to the beauty all around and you are left incapable of projecting your inner qualities to the world. The way others perceive you is a direct result of your inner dialogue. Your private thoughts and feelings aren't really that private, they affect everyone and everything around you. So, cultivate your self-worth and be proud of who you are.

Some people believe that loving themselves is arrogance. The truth is exactly the opposite. Arrogant people typically suffer from a suppressed low self-esteem. We must foster our inner value, it's imperative to our well-being, and it is part of our greatest gift to the world.

For love to exist, there must be a subject and an object partner relating harmoniously. Then, how can one love oneself? To fathom this, we must grasp that there exist dual characteristics even within one individual. The mind represents the higher self, and the body represents the lower self. When a man reaches perfection, his mind and body are in perfect harmony as subject and object partners, centering on his mind. However, since none of us have yet reached perfection, we all have a disharmonious relationship between our higher and lower selves. What separates a man able to love himself from one who is unable, is his ability to recognize and identify with his higher self.

Whatever you choose to identify with and focus on becomes your subject. If your lower self is your subject, then this will control your thought process. You have the power to shift this center over time. First off, you need to become aware that you are endowed with greatness. This may sound silly to you, since I don't know your name or address. Who am I to tell you that you have greatness in you? But at the same time, you already know that what I say is true. You already know that you have tremendous potential latent and hanging around, unrealized, deep inside. This is true for every person for whom the sun rose today, but the question is, what are you doing about it? What can you do about it? You can choose to embrace your higher self and access the hidden resources within you.

A clear illustration of the power of choosing to identify with your higher self is found in the story of Gollum, also known as Smeagol, from *Lord of the Rings*. This character is sharply divided within himself, to the extent that he has two personalities, one dominated by his higher self, and one completely surrendered to his lower self. The higher self, Smeagol, is kind, generous and sweet. The lower self, Gollum, is entirely consumed by dark desire for the Ring. At a critical moment in the story, when Smeagol begins to trust in the possibility of true friendship, Gollum reminds Smeagol that "You don't have any friends. Nobody likes you!" and that he is a liar, a thief, and a murderer. Gollum tries to subjugate Smeagol, rubbing his weaknesses in his face: "Where would you be without me? We survived because of me!" But in an epic showdown, Smeagol tells Gollum bluntly, "Leave and never come back!" Suddenly, Smeagol is alone! He jumps for joy, dancing and shouting, "We told him to go away... and away he goes ... Gone, gone, gone! SMEAGOL IS FREE!"

At the beginning of the story, Gollum/Smeagol has only one motivation: to regain possession of the Ring. But when Smeagol kicks Gollum out, Smeagol is free to be a genuine friend. If you haven't seen the movie *Lord of the Rings: The Two Towers,* then you can find this scene on the internet. It's worth watching as a powerful portrait of the battle each of us fights to maintain rule over our lower self by empowering and identifying with our higher self. It makes sense that victory in this battle is the beginning of self-love as well as the foundation for our ability to love others.

To love ourselves we must live in accordance with our higher values. We must define our core principles, and continuously act in a way that inspires our higher conscience. Since this is the foundation for self-love, and the love for others, we need tools for self-mastery. These strategies are covered more fully in chapters 10 and 12, but here I'd like to offer you an important technique to help you get in touch with your higher nature.

Get into the habit of pausing in the middle of the day. Relax and feel your breath. Listen to your heartbeat, feel your body pressing against the surface you are sitting on, your lungs expanding and contracting. Look at your hands, study their perfection. Softly massage your palm with the thumb and fingertips of your opposite hand. Pay attention to your gestures, and practice dignity and composure in everything you do. Be mindful of your actions, words and posture. Practice loving yourself daily, and consistently perform actions that are worthy of self-love. You will soon discover vast inner resources and realize how magnificent you are.

I'd also like to remind you not to dwell on your mistakes. Instead do your best to extract all the learning points from them, and then let them go. The world doesn't have time for you to dwell on your weaknesses, and neither do you, so put your higher self in the center, accept yourself, love yourself, and move onwards.

We all have light and darkness within us, but your intentions and focus determine what rules. A flashlight can easily light up a room painted black, but a thick layer of ink around the bulb can incapacitate the flashlight. What matters is what you give power to, what you identify with, and what you make your subject. Introduce light to the darkness rather than darkness to the light. This way you will always be encouraged. Don't think you are doing anyone a favor by undermining yourself. The world deserves your higher self and so do you. Of course, we don't need to boast about how great and almighty we are. Every person is great, every person is important, and as you like yourself more, you will find that you like other people more as well. In Aristotle's famous words, "All friendly feelings for others are an extension of a man's feelings for himself."

Agape - Love for Others

Just as we cultivate genuine self-respect and self-love through conscious efforts, we can consciously nourish the ability to see the good in others. Find ways to serve and care for others, and you will develop the confidence and strength to take the initiative in loving your woman.

The key to actualizing love is to prioritize the needs of others above our own. Many relationships fail because we forget this basic principle. Some people believe they're in love simply because they get triggered by someone's beauty, or because they feel happy or excited around someone. They believe that the source of love is found in their object. Thus, they try to extract happiness, satisfaction, or admiration from others. They are thus blinded from the richer expressions of love hidden right before their eyes.

People convince themselves they are acting out of love when they do a service for others, compliment them, kiss up etc., but deep down their motivation is to extract the quintessential nourishments that respect and affection provides. With this motivation, they lose access to true and lasting fulfillment. They might even end up frustrated or resentful because they aren't receiving what they need from their relationships. They blame others for absence of love in their lives, forgetting that love can't be received from others, only beauty. Love comes from within; it comes to us as we selflessly extend ourselves without a hidden agenda.

Whenever you give love to someone, you become a vessel filled with that which you impart. Every element, every gesture, every intention, and every thought you project to others, will pass through your spirit before it reaches theirs. This is the true secret to fulfillment in love. When our intentions and gestures are filled with life-giving elements, we become empowered and filled with the vitality of love. Rather than constantly seeking for love outside ourselves, we become a fountain that others can drink from. We will then naturally and effortlessly earn the trust and admiration of those around us.

We have no control over what we receive from others, but cultivating the ability to love, is entirely within our power. The key to becoming a perfect lover is to dedicate ourselves to the art of selfless giving. We must invest ourselves wholeheartedly, give and forget that we gave, and renounce the idea that others owe us for our service. This becomes possible when we realize that fulfillment from love is independent from other people's responses, and rather sprouts from the quintessential elements contained within the act of giving.

According to the laws of physical dynamics, as things move and expend energy, they lose momentum. Material wealth and physical energy diminish as you use them, but the energy of true love has no such limitations. As you extend your love to the people and even the things around you, you will find that your love expands and shines more and more brightly. As you extend yourself selflessly to the service of others, you will find that fulfillment, love, joy and even financial abundance will come chasing after you. Even if you try to escape, they will knock down your door and penetrate your life. The principles of the universe are founded upon the laws of attraction. When you become a beacon of love and beauty, these elements will seek you out, without any effort on your part.

Some people try to limit the force of love, by keeping it contained within their family or closest friends. This is certainly a step beyond trying to keep love to yourself, but ultimately, it's not enough. If you try to contain love it eventually becomes stale and empty. It's like containing water from a fresh spring or waterfall into a bottle. The water that has circulated and traveled for millions of years are now given a stamp with an expiration date. Love can't be contained, it is meant to flow and shine, and ultimately cover the whole earth. If you try to contain love within a limited sphere, it too will be stamped with an expiration date, and it will eventually wither. When you live for the sake of your family, you are filial, when you live for the sake of your nation, you are a patriot, when you live for the sake of the world, you are a saint.

True love is limitless. It is our expressions that are limited. The more we try to constrain our love, the more we are blinded to its hidden potentials. You can't love your sweetheart without seeing her quintessence in other women. You can't love your brother or your father without seeing something of them in the men around you. The greater your love, the more it binds you to the people around you, and even to the people from across the world. If you try to love yourself or your lady only, and repress this natural connection to other people, then your love will either become hollow, or it will become an elusive dream that can never satisfy. As Jesus said, "If you love those who love you, what credit is that to you?" If you try to keep love to yourself, or even within your family, it will slip away from you. The human race is one body, interconnected by various systems and sub-functions. Trying to sever yourself from the world is a recipe for your own demise.

People are created to live in harmony in the same way that organs of the body harmonize to form a whole person. Each of the organs in our body – the brain, the heart, the blood vessels, the skeleton – has a unique and essential function. The value of each organ is equal to that of the whole body because if one of them breaks down, all of them will. If a man loses even his little finger, we can say that he is no longer whole. This is also true with an engine. A bolt may not have the same function as the piston, but without the bolt, the engine falls apart. In other words, the bolt has the same value as the piston, because without the bolt the engine is practically useless.

Similarly, in our society, we all have a unique function to complement and bring joy to each other. Some people assume the position of leaders and others of supporters, but they all have the same purpose and value in that every person has the potential to give and receive love. Some positions are necessary to achieve a specific task, but each person has a unique and divine value. In fact, those who appear humble often end up changing history.

<u>When Loving Others is Hard</u>

Most of us know the importance of accepting and loving other's, but sometimes it seems impossible. We get blinded by our judgmental filters and self-centered dogmas, and anyone different from us appears as an enemy. Our lower selves deceive and cloud us from the beauty within them. It requires willpower and discipline to access a higher viewpoint and to silence the voice of our lower selves, but if we do so, we will naturally and consistently see people with the generous eyes of love.

Everyone has a story of how they ended up where they are, a history that shaped them, a pain and a hurt that led them to close their hearts. It's usually the people who are hardest to love who need it the most. They are used to people giving up on them. Don't be that kind of person. Don't give up because your efforts seem unappreciated or unreciprocated. Continue to love, even those who are difficult. Through this consistent practice you can break through any wall and touch the lives of even the most closed-hearted individuals. They might not respond to you with gratitude, or acknowledge you in any way, but if you don't give up, your love will eventually heal them. This same love will flow through you as well. Through this practice, you too will be transformed.

Love and hate are closely bound. They come from the same energy of love, yet, one of them is pure and the other is tainted. One of them has the power to heal you and bring a sparkle to every aspect of your existence, and the other will surely destroy you. Choose which type of energy you want to cultivate but consider that whatever you inflict on others must pass through you first. If you wish to inflict misfortune, then your poisonous thoughts will pass through your mind, and flow in your veins and soul, before they reach the other person. The same is true for love. When you love someone, that same love passes through you first, and you too will enjoy the rich benefits of its fruits. Every planet circulates around its own axis as well as the solar system. When you choose to embrace the practice of love, do it for others, but also for yourself.

Our emotions and intentions form a self-perpetuating cycle. When someone says the world is full of hate and others say the world is full of love, it's a reflection of what they allow to pass through their systems. What we receive from others affects us, but not as much as what flows from within. Jesus said it is not what goes into a man's mouth that defiles him, but what comes out from his heart. What we cultivate within is what colors our experience of life.

You will always find people who are difficult, but therein lies the greatest opportunity to expand your love. Loving people is a discipline to protect yourself as much as a discipline to benefit others. Instead of resenting people who frustrate you, consider them a gift and an opportunity. The truth is, anyone can love their friends. It takes much more effort to love those who disagree with you. Making the effort to love such people is the greatest practice of love. Remember that whatever you inflict upon others must go through you first, and whatever you project comes back to you.

Love for Creation

As we are discovering, becoming a better lover is not merely about putting our focus on a cute girl. It's about cultivating self-worth, investing in others, and even in appreciating the abundant beauty all around us. Only when we see beauty will we find love. So, open your eyes to the wonders around you. Extend your gaze to the sun in your eyes, and to the breathtaking scenery, vibrant life and delicious fruits offered by the natural world. Our adoration never goes out without effect, even if it is directed toward a simple flower. Think about how much impact your unspoken sentiments, your secret yearnings, have on your beloved. Cultivate your ability to remain in wonder for everyone and everything around you, and then bring this life-giving awareness and energy back to your girl.

When I spend time with nature, I feel enlightened. Ideas come to me, love flows through my heart, and a sense of peace and quietude settles inside me. Truly, nature is alive, and if we learn to relate to it, it can teach us many things. It changes us, opens us up to the love latent within, and even reveals its secrets to those who know how to look and listen. Most of the things I know about life, about the masculine and the feminine, about love and happiness, I have learned from nature. Nature, in its perfection, can be our greatest teacher and our most pristine source of inspiration.

I first learned to appreciate nature during my stay at a mountain retreat in La Cote d'Azur (South-France). During my stay, we got up at five o'clock each morning to prepare to welcome the sunrise. We started the day by cleaning up mentally and physically before embarking on the breathtaking hike up the mountain. On our predawn hike, we remained completely silent, focused on the sounds, sights and feel of the life around us as nature started to awaken. At the top of the hill we sat down by *La Rochette,* a mighty boulder, and we waited for the sun to rise. We spent an hour meditating, doing breathing exercises, listening to the birds singing, and trying to connect with all living things. As the sun finally appeared, we inhaled its light with love and gratitude. We remained seated for an hour after sunrise, enjoying the delicate first rays of morning light.

After meeting the rising sun, I was filled with a singular feeling of peace and contentment. It felt like I was walking on clouds the whole day. Meditating at dawn opened my eyes to the love, light, and beauty inherent in all of nature. I was filled with awe and wonder. I was blown away by this totally new and unexpected experience that was unlike anything I had even guessed to be real, even though I had lived through more than seven thousand sunrises at the time. Meals tasted better, people appeared happier, and everything I did for the remainder of the day seemed more enjoyable.

Nature offers us such gifts if we take the time to appreciate. If you sit down at the top of a mountain, or by the sea, to take in the sunrise one morning, you will know this to be true. The purity of the virgin rays that penetrates your skin at the break of dawn is so vibrant that it can heal your body, solve internal imbalances and cure sadness. When the sun has cleansed you, you no longer see problems. Your heart is open to the rich beauty of the natural world. You are free as well to see the splendor of life and the beauty of your lady.

The more you study and fall in love with nature, the more you unravel its mysteries. Day in and day out the sun sends light, warmth and love. It nurtures us, energizes us, comforts us and lights up our lives. The sun doesn't care if its love is reciprocated. It overlooks human hate, ignorance and our outrageous lack of gratitude, and sends its life-giving warmth and light all the same.

All of nature demonstrates this unchanging love. The trees and the plants remove our pollution, spiritually as well as physically. Day in and day out plants consume carbon dioxide and transform it into oxygen for us to breathe. The earth converts compost into beautiful trees, fruits, and flowers. And last but not least, fresh air and sunlight can turn resentment into inner peace. If you do not believe me, try taking a walk in nature next time you feel upset.

Back home in Norway, even the factories are nestled in among the fjords where the view takes your breath away. Wherever you may find yourself, you are close to stunning natural beauty. In the winter, though, the sun may not appear for weeks. Then you realize how gloomy, painful and depressing the world can be without the sun. But when summer finally rolls around, the sun never sets. A newfound joy covers the whole land. You must experience this; it's a peculiar phenomenon. Everyone suddenly seems vibrant and friendly. People who live in the North fully recognize the sun as the source of life and joy.

I consider the sun, the trees and the flowers my companions and greatest teachers, because they model the ideals and principles that I study and practice. If we could manifest even a tiny fraction of the love and wisdom that nature flaunts, we would surpass any earthly master. If we could embody the unconditional light of the sun, the faithful service of a plant, the richness and abundance of the ocean, and combine these with the supreme intellect and heart of a human being, we would reach the towering heights we have never reached but have all longed for. I wonder if you can understand and believe that nature has the power that I ascribe to it, but the more you study nature, the more you will uncover this divine truth for yourself. The powers of nature are magical. Spend time meditating on the glory of the forest, the light of the sun, the beauty of the flowers, and the majesty of the ocean. Eventually you will discover secrets that no other source can reveal.

Eros – Romantic Love

What defines a woman? What is her quintessence? Is her beauty defined by the smoothness of her skin or the fragrance of her neck? Is it found in the kindness in her eyes, the charm in her smile, the eloquence of her curves, or the softness in her voice? How about the movement of her hips as she walks, the gentleness of her touch or the warmth of her embrace? Yes, it's all these things. But there is something more, something the physical eye cannot see. Her true beauty is not found in exterior looks, outer qualities or even personality, but in an underlying principle that defines her femininity.

As time passes, our feelings for each other seem to fade. A pleasing figure ages or becomes old to us as the novelty of intimacy declines. Circumstances and disappointments may make us lose trust in each other. Our fascination with physical beauty and charming personalities fades away, but the beauty and brilliance of Yin, the feminine principle, knows no end. We must learn to see our girl beyond a pleasing figure and a charming personality, and part of an eternal principle. Just like the electron is irresistibly drawn to the proton and naturally forms a harmonious bond, when we discover the underlying feminine principle in our woman, and learn to embrace our own masculinity, our relationship will resonate with the cosmic laws more ancient than time.

Yin is the primordial principle, the perfect ideal, that all men search for in a woman. To know Yin, we must study all women, and seek the quintessence that defines their femininity. In coming alive to the feminine principle in all women, we can savor the value of our own. This principle is too great for words to describe, it must be discovered and experienced. When it touches you, its feels like a wave of beauty washing over your soul, accompanied by deep contentment because you realize that the purpose for which you were created is accomplished through Her, and only Her.

Within Yin, you will discover the beauty of a woman. Seek for it and you will find it. The fountain of the divine principle will never run dry, so the more you seek, the more you will find. When you discover this principle, you will understand true love. This is the key to becoming a true lover of women, and especially, of your beloved.

Many people believe that leaving behind a dull relationship to take on a new partner will enrich them. This is an illusion derived from a misunderstanding of Yin. The never-ending search for the perfect partner is bound to result in disappointments. You will keep finding the same flaws and challenges in each subsequent relationship, because external trappings can never satisfy us. Instead, we must dedicate ourselves to discovering Yin, and then uncover this principle within our lady. This is the true path to supreme fulfillment. Your beloved contains the essence of Yin. She alone holds the key to unlocking your greatest desire.

When we dedicate ourselves wholeheartedly to loving one woman, we allow ourselves the chance to mature beyond a childish and meager concept of love, and access the higher love manifested by the sun and all of nature. Your commitment creates a sanctuary to heal her faults, to draw out her potential, and to bring love into fulness. Only when you have tasted the depth of joy and sadness, of euphoria and despair, together with one woman, can you understand the rich qualities inherent in Yin. These qualities reveal themselves in the sanctuary and sanctity provided by genuine commitment and dedication.

Dedicate yourself to understanding the feminine principle. Search for it everywhere. If you pay close attention, you will soon discover that it exceeds your wildest imagination. Spend time studying women with the purpose of understanding your own. Each woman has her unique personality and vibration, but underneath lies the principle more ancient than time. This discovery is the unveiling of the true *Mysteries of Yin*.

Pathway to Mastery

Section 4

Section IV revisits the topics of the three previous sections and offers practical advice and methods to master the ideas discussed. Each of the remaining chapters respectively corresponds to the previous three sections.

Self-Mastery

Chapter 10

«The first and greatest victory is to conquer yourself»

~Plato

T he first section in this book was about self-change. We discussed how to see ourselves with clarity, compassion and vision, how to find our true calling, and how to build the confidence and skills to take on leadership. In this chapter we will revisit these concepts and develop a plan to obtain our goals. In addition, we will introduce specific methods to overcome the challenges we meet along our journey. This chapter is about self-mastery.

Before we can forge a plan to accomplish our vision, we must first accept that challenges will come to us, and that the higher our goals, the steeper the path ahead. Many people pour out their effort to avoid hardship; they hide, dodge and take long detours to avoid anything that looks unpleasant. They don't realize that obstacles represent opportunities to advance. If you study the lives of great men, you will soon realize that they all reached greatness by working through spectacular obstacles. Certainly, there are people who stumble into good fortune. But fortune is fickle, and ongoing success requires that we continue to mature. The only effective way to rise above our challenges is to foster our internal qualities.

This ideal is in contradiction to how many choose to live their lives. Most people try to overcome their challenges by changing or controlling their circumstances. This seldom works because the way we see, feel about, and experience our day-to-day reality is a reflection of our inner workings. Therefore, before we can work on improving our circumstances, we must first obtain mastery of our minds. When we can quiet the chaos within, and establish inner harmony, then clarity and peace of mind comes to us naturally. Furthermore, we will no longer be afraid of difficulties, but see them as a necessary and vital part of reaching our destination. Obstacles will feel more like muscle pain after a work-out, or like the stress of figuring out tough test questions, and less like staring at a hole in the hull of your ship when you are half-way across the Pacific. The first part of this chapter, then, is about appreciating challenges and even hardships. From there we will develop a specific plan of action to obtain our goals. Finally, we will cover specific practices to help us chart and maintain our course toward success.

Acceptance

The first step to overcome your challenges is to accept that they exist. When you are overwhelmed with pain, or in denial, you are not free to assess your situation and respond effectively. Acceptance does not mean that you give up or stop trying, it means that you see the situation for what it is and make peace with it. Only then can you work constructively. If you have a strawberry seed, and you are angry that you don't have a strawberry, then you may fail to recognize the value of the seed. Instead you should accept the fact that you don't have a strawberry and realize you have the potential to create one. When we accept the situation for what it is, and confidently decide to press through whatever obstacles lie ahead, then we are already half-way to victory.

Instead of being stressed or upset about your situation, perhaps a constraint you have, a personal limitation, or a difficult circumstance, choose to understand these things as given to you for a reason. This thought isn't just a philosophical belief to comfort us in tough times. It is instead a practical reality that you must appreciate if you want to thrive in the real world. Our generation is obsessed with seeking comfort at all cost. There is something to be said about sending boys into the wilderness to proclaim their manhood. Harsh circumstances mold us into better men, allow us to experience greater levels of joy, and prepares us to overcome future responsibilities with ease. An easy life is not an advantage. It's like a diet consisting of twinkies and coke. It gives an illusory sense of comfort, but it doesn't nourish us. If you always avoid challenges, you will live your life in fear, because you never develop the courage and skills to overcome them. Why not choose to say to yourself: "I will accept this challenge because I know that once I overcome, I will be stronger and wiser and able to take on even greater challenges in the future"

A great symbol of accepting and overcoming challenges can be found in how an oyster reacts to a grain of sand. Obviously, an oyster has no way to remove a grain of sand from inside its shell. Imagine the constant irritation in its delicate flesh. How terribly unpleasant! However, the oyster does not allow itself to get bent out of shape. Instead, with patience and diligence, it secretes a liquid that forms a soft shield around the irritating grit. Month after month it coats the sand until it becomes one of the great wonders of this world, an oyster pearl. The oyster doesn't rebel against its insufferable predicament, and it doesn't get depressed over its very limited faculties. Instead it goes to work and gradually overcomes the problem, with miraculous results!

Just like the oyster turning a grain of sand into a magnificent pearl, so our problems represent opportunities. The Chinese character for crisis is composed of two other characters, one meaning danger, and the other meaning opportunity. When crisis strikes, you have your best chance to achieve something out of the ordinary, and to become more than you would be if you stayed in your comfort zone. Great men are made, not born that way. It's not that you will become great despite your challenges, but because of them. This might sound shocking to you, but it's true. A great life is infused with obstacles and trials, and if you never experience hardships, you will never acquire the wisdom and potency to embrace a truly fulfilling life. Of course, life might beat you down, but success lies in whether you lose hope and give up or find a way to use your challenges as steppingstones.

Appreciation

"Let's rise and be thankful, for if we didn't learn much today, at least we learned a little. And if we didn't learn even a little, at least we didn't get sick. And if we did get sick, at least we didn't die. So, let us all be thankful."
~*Buddhist Proverb*

When you are faced with a challenge, the splendor of life is easily overshadowed. The simple joys that filled you with contentment suddenly seem lackluster and empty. Of course, nothing outside you has changed, but you have become preoccupied with your troubles. It's then easy to lose the courage and strength to deal with what's happening, and to sink into self-pity. Strength comes from the realization that our challenges are imbued with opportunities. Let this thought inspire you and lead you to an uplifting and productive mindset. Challenges have the power to cloud your world, so use your perception to pierce through the fog and expose the simple pleasures of life. This will give you traction to take up the fight and face your challenges dead on.

Our emotions are addictive. There are chemicals in our brain and in our blood that correspond to the emotions that we habitually entertain. Our established thinking patterns generate specific emotional states. To change these patterns, we must change our focus; we must mindfully redirect our thoughts and establish new behavioral patterns. Start by recognizing that self-pity is a total waste of time and realize that most of your worries in life are groundless fabrications of your mind. Your outlook and direction in life is shaped by your focus. If you focus on worries and hardship, this is what you will foster and create. If you focus on splendors and opportunities, this is what comes to you. Therefore, practice the skill of gratitude.

Give thanks for your health, your friends, your family, and the wonders of the natural world. Give thanks for your resources, your skills, and your joyous experiences from last week, last year, or last decade. Give thanks to the great masters of human history who propelled social, moral and spiritual progress, and for scientific insights and technology that shaped our civilization. There is an outlandish saying that our society is slowly decaying, and that life was better in the past. This outlook is provided by the same misguided focus we are trying to cure. Life is infinitely better today than it was a thousand years ago, or a hundred years ago, or even ten years ago. Human standard of living is exponentially flourishing. Conflicts, deceases and starvation is plummeting. Education and resources are at our fingertips like never before in history.

Get into the habit of honing your focus towards gratitude and opportunities. Get a journal, and every day write down things you are grateful for. Once you direct your thoughts to the things that make your life worth living, you develop an emotional and mental link to these things, and you will automatically create similar elements. This exercise will slowly alter your emotional and physical circumstance. When you have gained the ability to accept and appreciate your challenges in and of themselves and learned to see beauty in the direst of situation, then your convictions will be unshakable. Then you will be ready to draft your action plan.

The Action Plan

Now that we have learned to see our challenges as steppingstones, from a place of acceptance and appreciation, it's time to develop an action-plan and enter a higher realm of self-actualization. To execute the method, you will need your list of goals and visions discussed in Chapter 2.

Start by looking at your list and contemplate all the glorious dreams, virtues, goals and visions you have derived for yourself, and allow excitement and inspiration to fill you. You can choose a specific item or do them all at once. Next, you need to select a time frame for the completion of your objective. It could be less than a week, it could be a month or even five years or more. Make sure you choose optimistically but with some hint of realism. Remember you can use this method as many times as you like.

Step One: Your Victorious Future Self

Your imagination, your emotions, your memories and your creativity have tremendous power over your conscious and logical mind. When you master the skill of visualization, you can access the broader powers of your subconscious mind, and harness astonishing abilities of suggestion.

Start by accessing your higher self. Place your left hand on your forehead, and your right hand on the back of your head, to stimulate your blood flow. Close your eyes and access the inner resources of your mind. Embrace the man you know in your heart you were born to be, your true and perfect self. Experience his virtues, qualities, purity, strength and integrity. Step into his shoes, breathe in his air, smell the room you are standing in, listen to the sounds around you, and feel your body weight pushing against the surface. Truly embrace this higher state of consciousness.

Now, ask your higher self if your goal is worthy of your highest and noblest destiny. Listen with a disinterested, clean heart, and free yourself of preconceived notions or of strong personal desires. If you receive affirmation, then you can move forward with renewed confidence and purity of motivation. Remember, we must move boldly but also in harmony with our highest purpose, and with the universe, from which we draw our every breath and nourishment.

Next, begin your travel into the future. Embrace the reality that you have already gone through all the steps needed to gain the success you're striving for. Imagine vividly the thoughts and emotions going through your mind after you have accomplished your goal. Listen to the thoughts roaming through your mind and feel the emotions pulsing in your veins. Make this as real as you possibly can.

Breathe deeply and turn your mind's eye to the memory of your journey from this very moment until the completion of your chosen task. Visualize the trials you went through, the difficulties, and the glorious victories. When you have embraced your future self, proceed by asking yourself these three questions.

1. What were the most important tasks that led to your success?
2. What advice would you give to your novice self?
3. How did this experience change you?

As you ask yourself these questions you will soon realize that the answers to your personal advancement are already contained within you. Make sure you write down all the insights you gain from this exercise. You will use them to build your action plan. Remember you can tailor these guidelines and expand on the questions above. These three basic conversations will spark your imagination, and help you discover and get acquainted with your highest and noblest self.

Step Two: The Propulsion System

After you have received insights and ideas, developed a clear image of where you want to go, and visualized the journey to get there, it is time to draw up a practical strategy to realize your goals. Synthesize all the ideas and insights gained from your higher-self meditation and begin to develop a plan of action.

Create a timeline detailing the things you need to accomplish to meet your objective. Describe the key steps, your methods, and your time frame for completion. Seek advice and guidance along the way but learn to trust your intuition and the guidance from your higher self. You will find your feet in life more and more as you continue to refine your vision and assess your goals along the path.

A clear tangible image of where you want to go becomes a powerful force pulling you in the right direction. However, to create a proper propulsion system you also need a force pushing you away from where you don't want to be. Therefore, proceed by imagining what will happen if you don't venture into the rich journey you have planned for yourself.

Imagine yourself at your deathbed, contemplating all the things you did not experience in life, because you were too scared to venture into the unknown or to put in the necessary efforts. Experience the regrets of not having pursued your dreams, and of having sunk into fear, laziness and mediocrity. See your flawed self and use this sorry scene to galvanize your determinations to succeed. Hold these two poles, of where you want to go and where you don't want to go, clearly in your mind, and use them as inspiration to take the necessary steps each day.

Step Three: The Three Boxes

Now that you have a clear image in your mind of what you want to accomplish, a powerful system of motivation, and a detailed plan to accomplish your objectives, it is time to develop the discipline to fulfill the necessary steps each day. The method of the three boxes is designed to help you approach your daily goals in a way that inspires you.

Each morning, after completing my visualization, I open my notebook and draw three boxes. I name them A, B and C. Inside box A I write down the most important things I need to accomplish that day. This box contains the absolute essentials. I make sure I check off the items in this box as early in the day as possible. When I write my objectives in box A, I make sure it contains nothing less and nothing more than the tasks that I absolutely must accomplish that day. I make sure that this list is realistic, and that if I focus, I can surely fulfill each responsibility. Because it contains the bare essentials, I refuse to go to sleep until I have checked off each task in this box. I also refuse to be disappointed with my day, or consider it a failure, if I have done so.

Some days everything seems to go wrong, unexpected events come up, and our minds are overwhelmed with stress. Despite this, I always make sure that the few items listed in box A are always checked off before I go to bed. I've come to realize, after giving this a lot of thought over many years, that there is nothing more important to my success and happiness than completing these items. After I complete box A, I relax a little and allow myself to enjoy the day as it unfolds.

Box B contains important tasks that are less time-sensitive than those urgent responsibilities listed in box A. You should expect to be able to complete at least most of these items within the day if you are motivated, clear-minded, and unhindered by unexpected circumstances. Because you have fulfilled box A, you can already count your day a success. You can free your mind from the gnawing fear that you will never be able to get "everything" done. This is a much healthier way to tackle a challenging schedule.

Box C contains yet another category of tasks. It includes the goals you can accomplish if the day turns out perfectly. Each day you reach into this box is a day worthy of celebration as a personal success. As you become stronger as an individual and gain self-mastery, your productivity will increase, and you will find yourself reaching into this box more and more often.

∗∗∗

When you contemplate your list every morning, look at your action plan and your daily schedule. You will see they are in perfect harmony. Even simple tasks take on meaning when you recognize their part in helping you realize your dreams. Keeping this in mind will help you maintain passion and focus throughout the day. Discipline yourself to achieve your tasks according to priorities A, B and C, and you will gain momentum and endurance to reach your higher destiny. As we mentioned in Chapter 2 through the golf ball metaphor, simple but consistent daily disciplines will bring impressive changes over time.

Continuous Self-Mastery

Once you set sail towards a higher destiny, you will soon discover unexpected rough seas. The waves can strike you relentlessly and with enough force to knock you off course if you are not prepared. To ensure that you stay on course, you must have the necessary ballast. Your ballast primarily consists of your deep-rooted character and vision for life, but you can add extra weight with specific tools and methods. This section will present various methods and mindsets to help you stay true to your course.

Mental strength comes from our abilities to control our thoughts and emotions. Thoughts and emotions are like waves. They can be a powerful source of distraction and discouragement and can easily push us in the wrong direction if we are not mindful. The ability to control his thoughts and emotions is in many ways what separates a man able to stay true to his course from one who is easily lost in rough seas. Because this issue of command over our thoughts and emotions is so essential, we will cover this aspect of self-mastery in detail.

Master Your Thoughts

"Watch your thoughts, for they become words.
Watch your words, for they become your actions. Watch
your actions, for they become your habits. Watch your
habits, for they become your character. Watch your
character, for it becomes your destiny. What we think, we
become"

~Margaret Thatcher - The Iron Lady (2012)

Our destiny is ultimately controlled by our thoughts. Being able to effectively govern our thoughts can unleash hidden resources within us. To do so, we must first realize that our thoughts do not represent our identity, they are separate entities with a life of their own. This realization allows us to observe our thoughts from a 3rd person perspective, and to choose whether we listen to them or not. I would like to recommend a few techniques that you can use to tame your thoughts and emotions and bring them under the loving dominion of your higher nature. I encourage you to experiment and choose the ones that suit your personality and your circumstances.

The best way to control negative thoughts is to catch them in their infant stages, connect with your higher nature, and then redirect your attention towards more productive cognitive patterns. Whenever you find yourself entertaining destructive thoughts, such as those arising from self-doubt, jealousy, lust, hate, laziness, fear, or other lower impulses and distractions, interrupt them. Cut your thought process and redirect your attention to something beneficial. Take a breath and draw on the qualities of your higher self: serenity, compassion, kindness, passion, strength, gratitude etc. Your frame of mind will soon change as you continue to draw fresh inspiration from a higher level of awareness. This process requires strength of mind, but as you exercise this mental muscle, you will gradually be stronger.

Don't judge your thoughts or allow yourself to be angry because unpleasant thoughts or feelings come to your mind. Remember that you are not your thoughts, and choose to observe them with a peaceful attitude, as if you are watching a movie unfold before you. One method that helps me to distance myself from negative thoughts is to imagine them inside a picture frame or a book. I acknowledge them without judging them, I take some time to observe them, and then I thank them, as if they were the voice of a child who needs to be acknowledged even though their contribution isn't particularly helpful. Finally, I see myself flip the page, or swipe to the right, as I would do on a tablet. In other words, acknowledge your thoughts, regardless of what they are, thank them, and then dismiss them if they are not productive. Recognize that in themselves thoughts are harmless if you are in control, and deliberately choose to make room for a more constructive thought pattern.

Inevitably we occasionally end up absorbed by a negative thought pattern. If we don't interrupt our thoughts at their infant stages, they will multiply and grow until they discolor our entire reality. At these times it is hard to wake up to the beauty of the natural world, and to draw on fresh inspiration. We may become depressed, hopeless, and imprisoned by the belief that there is no solution to our current predicament. I would like to suggest a few methods that you can use in moments like these.

The first technique has to do with intently washing your hands. The symbolism of washing away impurities from your hands has surprising effects on your consciousness. Wash your hands intently under warm running water and say to yourself: "As I wash away the stains from my hands, may the confusion and distress from my mind be washed away as well." Softly massage your hands under the water and regain a purity and focus of mind.

A second technique is to dispel your stress and worries into the soil. The soil has magical effects. It takes compost, rotten produce, cow manure and deceased carcasses, and over time transforms it into brilliant flowers, vegetation and fresh fruits. There is no better symbol for healing internal balances in your mind and giving light to fresh inspirations. Go into your garden and put your hand in the soil. Pronounce to the soil: "Please accept the compost of my mind, my destructive thoughts and negative energy, and convert it into brilliant expressions of beauty and emerging life." This sounds unorthodox at the very least, but it has truly magical effects.

The last method I will recommend is going to the sunrise. I have continually expressed my fascination for the sun; there is no greater source of inspiration and healing. The light of the sun contains all the elements necessary to sustain human life and our planet. Every morning, all of nature waits in eager longing for the rising of the sun, because it is natures source of energy and revival. Wake up in the morning and prepare for the sunrise. Convince your mind that you are about to experience the greatest healing power in the natural world.

Meditate before the sunrise, and as it emerges from the horizon, drink from its brilliant rays. Feel the light of the sun dispel your stress, sadness and confusion, refresh your spirit, and reset and revitalize your mind. Visualize your solar plexus filled with the light of the sun. Cover your right nostril and breathe in through your right. Imagine your body being flooded with light, and visualize your breath and your solar plexus as radiating with a steady, bright glow. Let the light work within your body as you hold your breath for 15-20 seconds, then cover your left nostril and slowly exhale from your right. Let all your worries and tensions be carried from your body as you exhale. Repeat this exercise by alternating your nostrils, until you have filled your spirit with light, dispelled your worry, restored inner balance, and drawn fresh inspiration from your higher self. Doing this exercise consistently, can have marvelous effects on your inner consciousness.

As you learn to quiet your mind, you will develop the ability to rise above the negative thoughts that inevitably enter your mind in the course of self-improvement. If you want to achieve your goals, you must be consistently able to meet your responsibilities with a clear mind and a peaceful heart. That kind of consistent strength comes to you only if you can tame your destructive thoughts and emotions. Be mindful of the thoughts or feelings that draw you into depression, anxiety, fear or loneliness. Recognize that these negative thought patterns carry no real truth. Most of your worries never happen, but even while facing a real problem, negative thoughts will not help you. Only when you have freed yourself of the bondage of a negative thought spiral can you unleash the hidden resources within you. The truth is that you have everything you need to succeed, but in order to reach for your goals, you need to tap into the hidden resources provided by a clear mind.

Master Your Emotions

It's common to meet people who make their emotions their god. They declare, "But that's how I feel!" as if their feelings are sacred and they can allow no further discussion. They are not attentive, and they fail to see that following their emotions blindly can lead them down dangerous paths. Similarly, people who complain that they are depressed, frustrated, or angry, seldom take time to investigate why they feel the way they do. They do not look for an alternative way of looking at their situation. Instead they say: "That's how I feel, and there is nothing I can do about it." What nonsense!

We all have emotions, but what differentiates people is how we choose to respond to them. A feeling of resignation can easily turn into resentment, depression, and even hate if we are not careful. However, it can also lead us to change our behaviors and become more effective. It depends on our response to our initial emotion. No matter what emotions come up, it is imperative to investigate them and to deal with them in an optimal manner. Changing your emotional pattern can drastically change your life.

An important tool in developing emotional control is to become aware of our tipping points. Whenever we are about to fall off the cliff into emotional breakdown, there is always a warning sign appearing first. Learn to read yourself and recognize the signs that you are about to lose control. It requires self-control to resist the temptation to just let go. You may feel justified in wallowing in your negative feelings, and you may be tired of fighting them. Even so, learn to recognize when you are heading into an emotional storm, and at that moment, pause, breathe, and head for safe harbor. Utilize some of the techniques mentioned here, or go for a walk, take a nap, or turn to one of your cherished avocations. Diffuse the situation the way you might do if you were taking care of a little kid about to have a tantrum. Then you will be able to get in touch with your higher self and come back to face your challenges with renewed peace and strength.

Learning to govern your emotions is about more than being able to clear your mind. It's about learning to understand your body and the messages it brings. Emotions arise from various sources; they are the manifestation of the energies circulating within and around you. They may come from your thoughts attracting a particular set of spiritual energies, or they may come from the people you surround yourself with, from people you pass on the street, or from hidden principalities in the natural world. We can never have complete control of the energies surrounding us, but we can learn to control the emotions that get processed through our bodies and minds.

Emotions are energies moving in our bodies and they often carry valuable messages. Whenever an emotion surprises you, be it wild exhilaration, deep resentment, or even a gentle feeling of anticipation that you might otherwise ignore, take time to investigate it from a 3rd person perspective. Feel how it moves around your body, imagine its color and texture, and familiarize yourself with it as much as possible. Doing this will help you know your emotions intimately and allow you to guide them into something beneficial rather than destructive.

Emotions are only energy currents. Whether they lead to bad or good outcomes depends on you. For example, imagine that you experience an unusually pure and genuine joy washing over your soul. If you are not careful, that joy will simply dissipate like morning dew. However, if you understand the value of this precious sensation, then you will make the effort to retain it and magnify it. You must focus your awareness, both mentally and emotionally, and allow the joy to fill your body and penetrate your soul. Resentment on the other hand can be a warning to you. It must be resolved and healed, or it will poison you and damage your relationships. If you meditate on your emotions, you will discover a deeper awareness. This mindfulness allows you to embrace and channel your emotions and ride on their momentum rather than struggling against their pull. If you neglect to work on your emotions, then you will lose much of the joy of living as many great moments pass you by. You will also be at the mercy of festering problems that would otherwise be minor ordeals.

Detach Yourself

The road towards self-mastery is ultimately a road to detachment. Detachment from desires, emotions, and even material comforts. Detachment does not mean owning nothing, it means that nothing owns you. This is the only path to true ownership. Detachment means you are no longer a slave to whims. For instance, you can go for days without food without panic or fear. If you find yourself in a time of famine, while others are looting and pillaging, you'll be able to keep your calm knowing that everything is temporary, and a test of mother nature through time. You will no longer depend on your material possessions for self-confidence or for comforts, instead you will be able to truly enjoy them as a supplement rather than a necessity. Likewise, you will not be controlled by your thoughts, emotions or desire, but rather enjoy them from a place of mastery.

The best practice of detachment is to experience occasional abstinence from physical pleasures, and even physical needs. If you can go without these things for a predetermined length of time, then you will be better able to control your appetites day by day. You will also come to trust your ability to endure the privation or hardships that arise in this highly unpredictable life. The goal is to become detached from your compulsions and physical needs, so that rather than being dominated by them, you can savor their fruits from a place of strength and awareness.

We are all born with a natural drive, a powerful life force. This drive is what gives us inspiration, motivation, passion, power and courage to overcome obstacles and pursue happiness. This is an inherent force that rises naturally from within and explains why children and young adults are often filled with unstoppable vitality. Sadly, many of us lose touch with this inherent inspiration because our lives are too comfortable. Whatever we desire, we indulge in, and so we rob ourselves from the opportunity to build our inner drive. If whenever we are hungry, we eat, and whenever we are thirsty, we drink, and whenever we are sleepy, we sleep, we never really connect with the force of our inner drive, and we lose our zest for life. Settling for a mediocre life safely surrounded by creature comforts robs us of that spark of motivation to pursue true fulfillment.

One effective way to free ourselves from our comfort zone and to regain our vitality is to occasionally deprive ourselves of what we want. If you consciously deprive yourself of a luxury, or even a necessity, for a period, it builds will power and character strength. I recommend you experiment with overcoming lack of food, lack of sleep, lack of warm water in the shower, etc. Practice abstaining from sex, social media, TV, meat, coffee, or chocolate. Whenever you deprive yourself of something you depend on for comfort, a strong emotional resistance will well up inside you to try and stop you. However, as you calm your mind and settle your fears, you soon realize that you are in complete control of your desires. This realization will strengthen your resolve to overcome many other challenges in life.

It's easy to let our desires and fears control us. If we never deprive ourselves of anything, we live in constant fear of losing what we have. It is only when we resist our desires that we find the strength to master them. When we're no longer driven as a slave by our desires, then we can finally take full ownership of our bodies and our properties, and truly enjoy the objects of our desire.

What is it that you believe you cannot live without? Sex? TV? Video games? Food? Coffee? What are you afraid of losing? Whatever it is, decide to live without it for a short time. It is perfectly healthy to go a few days without food. If you're in good health and you prepare a little ahead of time, you can go several weeks without food and be much better for it. I am not saying you need to be extreme in any way, but why not experiment a little? Swear off coffee for a month, if it's your habit to drink it every day, and see how you cope. Chances are it will be difficult at first. You may feel like your desires are running you over like a train. But be patient and withstand your urges. Doing without something you rely on is like shaking a glass filled with grains of sand; it looks like a torrential storm inside the glass, but very soon the sand will settle. Give yourself a little time and take a few deep breaths. You will soon find your peace. When this happens, you will have acquired true mastery over your desires. You will no longer be afraid of losing things, and you will be free to embrace adventure and enjoy opportunities, even if they include somewhat frightening changes. You will be free to pursue your goals, and confident in your abilities to achieve them.

The men who live in constant plenitude, who get anything they want, and indulge in anything they get, become weak-minded. Whenever a temptation comes to them, they surrender their dignity and principles in order to satisfy their craving. They have a hard time protecting and nurturing a family because they are unable to sacrifice their own needs for the sake of others. They are easy to control, because as soon as you take away something they crave, they are unable to function. Control over your desire is the key to enduring the sacrifices inherent in being a provider and protector for your family. Love requires us to live for the sake of others. Because you have developed the self-control needed to sacrifice yourself for others, you will be able to taste the fulfillment that only love provides.

Master your Fear

If you set high goals and go after your dreams, you will have to face daunting challenges. When the real hardships of life hit you, even an arsenal of tools and techniques will not keep you afloat. The only thing that remains is courage. In the end it's your courage that gets you far in life. Developing courage is not easy. It usually comes as a result of overcoming obstacles. In the end however, it's up to you to decide that your fear is less important than your dreams. So, how do we muster courage?

I remember going to the amusement park as a kid, and I was always terrified of the big rides. One day however, I said to myself, "the heck with it!" and I headed for the scariest ride. After that, nothing was scary anymore, and I was finally free to enjoy any ride in the park. I had found my courage on that first big ride, and with that courage, the tough rides became exciting!

Franklin D. Roosevelt once said that we have nothing to fear but fear itself. Fear binds us, paralyzes us and keeps us from pursuing our dreams, and it often has nothing to do with reality. It also keeps us from seeing opportunities and overcoming our challenges. With courage we can take on any challenge and find it exciting.

I have often mentioned that we must never flee from challenges. Challenges build courage, and with courage we become stronger. When we develop the habit of acting on courage rather than fear, when we stand toe to toe with a challenge, the challenges become intriguing. We begin to welcome them and salute them for making our lives interesting. It is the consistent ability to meet challenges well that eventually leads to success.

There are many methods and techniques available to cope with life's challenges, but in the end, they are just training wheels. Ultimately, you must depend on the force of your will, on your maturity, and on your courage. Sometimes, it's best to let go of your training wheels all together and head out into the wide world in search of trials and all manner of adventures. This is where you find courage. Instead of going into escape mode whenever you feel afraid or uncomfortable by grabbing your phone or remote control, face your fear. Go deep within yourself and find the light within you, meditate and draw strength from the true source of courage, and break free from the chains that hinder you from reaching your true potential.

You can find your inner strength by drawing courage from your forefathers. Realize that your lineage is filled with champions. Sometime long ago your forefather stood on a dark, bloody battlefield with a sword in his hand, ready to fight for his country and for his woman. Not only did he risk his life to protect his woman, but he was victorious, at least long enough to have a son. That son became the father of another champion, and another, and another. You are proof that your bloodline is filled with champions, because it survived the hardships and bloody moments. All throughout history, throughout plague and war and many lesser tragedies, your bloodline survived, so that you could live. And what was your fear again?

Closing Remarks

A man's ability to conquer the world depends on his ability to conquer himself. On the path of life, great hardships and trials are inevitable, and our ability to stay true to our course is what determines our level of success in life. Visualizing a concrete goal and then developing a detailed plan to accomplish it, is necessary to bring your dreams to reality. However, even a perfect plan does not prevent us from having to face trials and endure hardships along the way. In fact, the greater our aspirations, the greater the challenges that await us.

Whether we live in the pursuit of excellence or a life in mediocrity, we cannot escape hardships. The hardships we face in pursuing our dreams include taking on responsibility, taking risks, working hard and enduring the related stress. The hardships we face in living a life of mediocrity are the consequences of settling for less. The jobs we take will be less stressful, but also less exciting and less rewarding. The girl we attract will join us in our mediocrity, and may disappoint us, or if not, she will be disappointed in us. We will experience emptiness, sadness and regret, because we will have chosen to deny our potential, our inner drive, and our inner truth. Ultimately, it is up to each of us to choose the hardships we prefer. It is my wish that you choose the former, and that you are now equipped with the necessary insights, tools and methods to get started.

Intimacy

Chapter 11

«Women speak two languages — one of which is verbal»

~William Shakespeare

S ection two explored the yearnings, desires, and special qualities of women. We studied harmony and we made sense of a woman's lovely yet unexpected ways. We discovered a new perspective on beauty, that love is its precursor, and that the qualities of a perfect lover centers on his ability to perceive and nourish the beauty within his beloved. Understanding her, and seeing her, is the foundation for a passionate love life. The next step is learning how to communicate. In this chapter we will develop the art of expressing and receiving love within the ebb and flow of the energies within and between us. It's time to explore the art of intimacy.

The spoken word is only one of the many rich languages that can spark fire and bring life into a relationship. There is a plethora of ways to build intimacy and to demonstrate affection. You could think of this chapter as a phrasebook for the foreign traveler. The guidelines suggested will help you navigate the new and famously mysterious world of the feminine heart and mind. But as with any other language, proficiency comes through experience, practice, and full immersion.

Speaking without Words

Body language is the secret tongue of intimacy. When you communicate without words, you convey your love in a richer, more personal, and more spiritually profound way.

Let me draw you an image:

Your woman comes out of the shower looking beautiful. Her skin is radiating and her feminine curves beckon to you from beneath her towel. Seeing your beloved stirs joy in your heart and floods you with passion. As you look at her face, your smile calls to her, and whispers affection from under your breath. You move your eyes slowly down her body noticing every detail of her pristine feminine form. All the way to her toes, and back up to her face. When you reach her eyes, you smile at her again with a slightly more mischievous look. You stretch out your hand to invite her to your lap, to the beginnings of an unfolding adventure.

Mastery of non-verbal communication has the power to unravel mystical adventures and deepen the connection between you and your beloved. When your gestures and gazes are imbued with subtle tenderness, you can communicate a rich story beyond words. A woman's expansive emotional vocabulary allows her to extract every possible intended meaning from this gentle yet potent exchange. Her imagination opens a world of possibilities when triggered through simple specific gestures. If you think I'm exaggerating, then read one of the romance novels that women so enjoy, detailing all the romantic little gestures of the central male character. The expression in your eyes and the mischief in your smile need no explanation or introduction, and without a single word or even the slightest touch, you can make her feel like running into you. Contrast the previous story with someone, oblivious to non-verbal communication, who barely looks at her before calling out in a casual or rough voice, "Hey, you look great, do you want to have sex?" It's easy to guess that she will be too busy or have a headache. He will have ruined the mood in 5 seconds flat.

When you master non-verbal communication, you can create a conspiracy between you and your woman, an atmosphere that isolates the two of you from the rest of the world, because you are the only ones who truly know what is happening beneath the surface. Your language is subtle, and your messages are only perceivable to the two of you.

Non-verbal language is like any other language; it takes practice and dedication to master it. It's not easy to explain how it works, because it's different for each person, different for each couple. It's like a code that develops as you come to know each other's cues and idiosyncrasies. The more you look for her subtle unique features, and the more you practice drawing her out with your eyes, the sooner you will master a language beyond words. Your bond will strengthen, and you will feel an intimate and hidden connection even when other people are nearby. With that said, there are a few essentials to consider as you learn this new way of getting to know each other.

A Tender Gaze

You may tell your girl a hundred times each day how beautiful and special she is to you, but it is your eyes that can truly communicate this message. You may say it constantly, but if you don't gaze at her from time to time, she will never truly believe you. To feel precious, she must sense that you take delight in her. Many men fail to look at their lady because they are unaware of the power of a look, and that through a single glance you can communicate your ardent adoration. Through the expression in your eyes, you can make her feel protected, important, beautiful and treasured.

Whenever your woman walks into the room, put everything aside for a second to take her in with your eyes. This takes only a second, but through this little glance, you confirm for her that you take delight in her. That's enough to show her she is more interesting to you, and more captivating, than anything else in the world at that moment. You don't have to say anything, because this gesture speaks volumes. A woman is intuitive, she can gain a world of inspiration through your eyes upon her and create a lush story from that flash of inspiration.

Your eyes can communicate a world of thoughts, ideas, emotions and intentions when you develop the language of your gaze. What often

160

separates a man who appears to be empty inside, and one who radiates charm and vitality, is his ability to communicate through his eyes. By communicating with your eyes, you can invite your woman into the rich rain forest of your inner world, flush with emotions, experiences and visions that the two of you alone will know and claim.

Having eye contact does not mean staring at her intensively. Looking directly into someone's eyes is something you do at job interviews to be polite. When you look into your sweetheart's eyes, you should expand your range of view to cover her whole being. This way of seeing her is an expression of the delight you feel when you take in the beauty of her face, and the subtle differences of expression in her features. You show that you truly care about what's going through her mind and heart. By observing her you can notice the subtle changes, the little ways that her expressions alter like the clouds and sunlight as they move across the sky. These small differences reveal her moods and emotions and betray her secret thoughts.

An Enchanting Smile

Smiling can convey a whole range of meaning. You can smile in a tender way, a goofy way, a sensual way, a playful way, an innocent way, a compassionate way and so on. Learn to master these various expressions, and you will command yet another language through your smile alone.

Many people smile in an artificial way, as a form of being polite, like shaking hands. This kind of smile is unnatural because it's just a social convention, not an expression of true feeling. Your face naturally reflects your emotions and state of mind, but if you habitually force a smile, then you limit your freedom to radiate the sincere joy that comes into your heart. All your smiles become the same, and to a sensitive observer, they are dull and empty. Practice letting your emotions flow freely and allow them to shine through in natural expressions on your face. You will soon learn that you are capable of effectively conveying a wide range of emotions and intentions through your smile. The wider your emotional register, the more flavor is added to your presence, and the more intriguing you become.

A Calm Demeanor

Many people who experiment with becoming more expressive end up overdoing it. Becoming a better non-verbal conversationalist does not mean being overly expressive, but rather it's about developing an awareness of your body language and facial expressions and bringing them into harmony with the natural flow of your emotions. This authenticity of expression through your body has nothing to do with acting out your emotions as a stage actor might, using clearly visible gestures for the sake of his audience. People who are overly expressive tend to look insincere, attention-needy and foolish. So, remain calm and composed. Then, as the natural currents of your inner state move through you, you will communicate with sincerity, richness and depth.

An Irresistible Charm

Have you ever noticed the irresistible pull of a small child? By simply toddling into the room, or by offering a simple smile or a laugh, they can melt the hearts of even the stingiest soul. If you can embody and practice the charm of small children, you can swoon any lady effortlessly.

A child's charm comes from their innocence, transparency, and self-acceptance. A child has nothing to hide, because their conscience is clean. You can attain a similar freedom if you resolve whatever troubles you, mend your rifts, and forgive yourself of your flaws. Of course, we can't be perfect, but we can live a life of self-purification day by day, and then be generous with ourselves. In so doing we can return to a state of innocence and be free to shine as small children do.

The second thing that makes children irresistible is their sincerity. Anything a small child says or does comes straight from the heart. When they smile, they smile naturally, and with their whole being. They are free to be themselves, and never worry about making a good impression. Their simple honesty puts us at ease because we don't have to wonder what they're really thinking, or what their hidden motives may be. It's refreshing to be around children, it's easy to connect with them, heart-to-heart, and so we feel enriched and unburdened, even if no words are spoken. People do silly and outrages things around children, things they would normally never do, because they are free to embrace their inner child.

162

If we can embrace the qualities of a child, we can spark life and authenticity into our interactions. Of course, we want to keep our dignity, but the spontaneity and self-acceptance that young kids have is a great model for us, all the same. Approach your lady with the charm of a child, and you will project a genuine, uncomplicated presence that refreshes her and puts her at ease.

A Magical Touch

Women know all about the language of touch, but most men are oblivious. Some men only associate touch with a sexual encounter. But a touch can communicate so many things. It can say "I desire you," but it can also say, "I am here for you," or, "Are you OK?" "Listen, this is important," or, in a teasing way, "You are such a dork." But the most central effect of a touch is to show that you are present, that you are invested in the interaction, and that you are intimate with each other. Using touch can be one of the most effective ways to build trust and intimacy in a relationship.

My initial idea for this section was to list all the different ways to touch a woman, and to explain the significance of each touch. But the truth is, *where* you touch a woman is of lesser importance. As you learn to utilize the power of touch as a tool to communicate and build intimacy, you will quickly understand how your lady responds to various types of touch. A massage, a kiss, a hug, a touch, a tap, a stroke, a scoop into your arms, all stimulate an emotional response when done correctly. What is far more important than *where* you touch or even *how* you touch, is the underlying energy currents that your touch transmits.

Two men can touch a woman at the exact same spot and stimulate entirely different responses. What makes the difference is the life and the energy imbued in their touch. Before you touch your lady, whether in a sensual way or to build closeness, bring your attention to your hands. Send warmth and energy to your palm and the tips of your fingers. If this is new to you it may sound strange, but as you practice doing this you will feel your hands start to heat up and radiate an energy that encapsulates the very essence of your masculine life force. This is the energy a woman truly longs for; your touch is simply a mechanism to transmit this energy to her.

Practice generating energy and warmth through your hands and then experiment with touching her. Don't be a fool (like most other men) by jumping straight to her sexual regions. Use your touch as a mechanism to build emotional intimacy. Allow time for her juices to flow by touching all her other sensitive regions. As you obtain mastery of this skill, practice generating that same energy through other channels: your lips as you kiss her, your heart center and solar plexus as you embrace her, and your sexual organ as you make love to her. Intimacy is all about generating energy. It is energy that creates ecstasy and emotional oneness between you and your lover. So, learn to exercise this sacred skill, and you will see your love-life transformed.

A Silver Tongue and A Golden Ear

Your words are a reflection of the divine principle. The functions of your mouth used to make sounds symbolizes the interactions of Yin & Yang, and your words are the fulfillment of the four-position foundation. Your lips (Yin) unite with your tongue (Yang), and through their harmonic interactions, they create sounds and words (Union). This interaction mirrors the principle used to create all things in nature. Your words have magical powers. They can uplift, create, transform and rebuild. Our civilization is built on words. Learning to communicate well has profound effects on the quality of your life and relationships.

Most people who learn to become better conversationalists focus on their delivery. They seek to improve their stories, their words and their presentation skills (Yang). However, effective communication requires that we fuel the creative harmony and circular motion of the Yin & Yang dynamic. We must learn to speak, yes, but more importantly, we must learn to listen. We need a silver tongue, and a golden ear.

Choose your Words

Your words have tremendous power. They can heal inner deceases, uplift your consciousness, inspire personal or societal change, and even transform your physical circumstances. They can also shatter and destroy relationships, your outlook on life, and even societal progress. Therefore, be careful with your words, and learn to use them as a tool to inspire and build intimacy. Develop sensitivity to your situation and audience. The same message can stimulate entirely different responses depending on the words you use. Practice mindfulness of your words, and you will progressively discover which words uplift and inspire, and which words leave conflict and chaos in their wake.

Words are commands that stir energy in motion all around us. They have the power to bring life and death. We are descendants of the Creator of the cosmos, who spoke life into existence. We possess the same creative qualities, and we create limitations or opportunities from the words we habitually pronounce. Refrain from using phrases such as "it's killing me", or "this makes me sick", because they have the power to manifest. Restrain from excessive cursing and restrain from using words born from doubt, anger or fear. Choose words that empower and uplift, reconcile and heal, and you will soon see your inner life and physical circumstance transform.

Conversation Styles

To communicate effectively in a relationship, we must understand that men and women have different communication styles. Men usually speak with a specific purpose in mind; they want to remind you to buy milk, explain how a transmission works, find out the scores from last night's soccer game, and so on. It's natural for them to ponder the things they want to say, and then formulate a specific statement or question. A woman's thought process is entirely different, she can easily communicate without any obvious purpose at all. She may not even know the purpose of the conversation until after it's over! Her thought process consists of simultaneous function from both hemispheres of her brain. It is complex and enhanced by powerful emotions and imbued with creative and analytical nuances concurrently. Sometimes, women talk in order to think. Also, they enjoy talking for its intrinsic value. They see it as an expression of trust and affection to confide in you, and as a way to invest in a relationship. So, gentlemen, I suggest that when your woman furrows her brow with concentration and launches into a meandering explanation of the pave-stones of Lima, that you fasten your seat belt and prepare to appreciate the scenery for the duration of the ride.

To the question: "What did you do today?" a man might answer, "We went over to our friend's house and had dinner. It was cool." A woman might answer, "Well, let me see... First, we did X, then we did Y, and Z, and then we went over to our friend Hannah's house, you know the Swedish girl that just moved here from Kansas, the one that's married to the German guy with the short brown hair, and has two kids, Nathan and Jeremy. She just got this beautiful new vase. You know the renaissance style, like the one we saw at Ikea last week. For dinner we had this amazing turkey with apple and mustard-sauce. I thought it was a bit risky to play with the spices the way she did, but you know that girl has always been a bit on the risky side. Did I mention she is Swedish? It was amazing. OMG, and their new dining table!...blah blah blah."

In conclusion, men and women often use communication for different purposes. Men transmit a specific, well formulated message with a clear agenda, while women might use talking to help them think, build relationships, clear away pent up emotions, relive an experience, and of course, to annoy men... It is important to be aware of these differences so that we can communicate in a way that enhances our connection. Sometimes we need to just be there for her and listen even if the conversation seems meaningless. It's a simple way to enhance our intimacy. We will also learn about her inner world, and perhaps a bit about renaissance vases.

Listening

A great conversationalist is someone who makes you feel included and excited by the interaction. He knows how to direct the conversation to keep you engaged, and he's curious about your ideas and perspectives. He is fascinated by you, he makes you feel heard, and he infuses excitement into the interaction by his enthusiasm and curiosity. This ability is acquired by skillful listening.

Listening is the critical component in skillful communication. It requires patience, clear perception of people's cues, and the ability to utilize curiosity and dive into someone's inner world. You must listen with more than your ears; listen with your eyes to notice the subtle changes in her facial expressions and body language and listen with your heart to feel the energy projections circulating within the interaction. Remember the exercises we studied in Chapter 7 and use it to find a deeper intimacy and to spark life into your exchanges. Communication can be more than the pragmatic exchange of words, it can be a dance, a courtship, a way to develop intimacy, and a way to dive into someone's inner world and develop a common vision. In dance, we must harmonize with the movements and intentions of our partner. Communication is the same way.

Many men struggle with conversation because they don't know what to talk about. They wonder what subjects are interesting, and what to do when they run out of things to say. In their frantic search for the right words and topics, they end up neglecting the girl. They become absorbed with themselves and fail to engage and notice her. Sometimes the most powerful exchanges are found in silence. If you don't know what to talk about, then why say anything at all? Instead, listen to her, watch her speak, and connect with your curiosity and excitement for her. Get in tuned with your love for her and allow this hidden energy to circulate between you. If you feel nervous in moments of silence, then prepare ahead of time. Relax your mind and heart, return to the feeling of joy, and allow yourself to taste the beauty of intimacy, without saying a single word.

Small Acts of Kindness

Words are important. However, sometimes the best way to express your love is to show it. It's not enough to tell your girl that you love her; she needs to see it in everyday affirmations through acts of kindness and affection. Certainly, we express our love by providing for her, ensuring her safety, meeting her physical and emotional needs, caring about her loved ones, and sacrificing ourselves for her benefit, however, small acts of kindness can act as icing on the cake to the larger and more fundamental contributions we do for her. Communicating affection doesn't always require grandiose gestures that break the bank. Just as in the case of the non-verbal and verbal communication, your success lies in subtle but persistent expressions over time.

One of my favorite fictional characters tells of his faith in little kindnesses in the movie *The Hobbit*. Gandalf explains that his mentor Saruman, who will become corrupt later in the series, "believes that it is only great power that can hold evil in check. But that it is not what I've found. I've found it is the small things, every act of normal folk that keeps the darkness of at bay – simple acts of kindness and love."

167

The world is saved through small consistent acts of kindness, and the same rings true for interpersonal relationships. You don't always need to offer extravagant gifts, but make sure that you pay attention to your woman, and show your affection through small, everyday gestures. Wake up each morning committed to do at least one small act of kindness for your woman that day. Below are a few suggestions.

Buy her a flower – You don't always have to buy her a diamond ring, or a whole bouquet of flowers. Instead, buy her one flower, or a small gift every once in a while. This continuous effort is more romantic than the grand gift that comes only once in ten years. Come home one day after work with a flower in your hand and tell her, "I walked by a flower shop, and it made me think of you." Then pull her towards you, hold her tight, and whisper in her ear how much you adore her. That's all you need to do to make her day. It doesn't always have to be flowers. When you are at the store bring back her favorite drink or snack, buy her new earphones if she needs them, or perhaps a special shampoo or perfume. Make sure to let her know that you bought it just because you thought about her. The validation she gets from knowing that you think about her throughout your day is more precious to her than the gift. When she eats the chocolate you gave her, it's not only the candy she will taste, but the flavor of your love, and the memory of your kiss that day. Don't be disappointed if she doesn't show appreciation right away. If you continue to give her small tokens of appreciation without expecting any particular response, she will eventually warm to your persistent love. She will tell all her friends how generous and loving you are, and then their men will be in trouble!

Invite her on a date three weeks from now – Inviting her on dates is essential. Even if you have been together for years, especially if you have been together for years. Many men make the mistake of trying to surprise their woman, planning a fancy secret evening to sweep her of her feet. Sometimes it works, but other times it doesn't. Perhaps she happens to be having a bad day, perhaps she is not prepared, or perhaps she has other plans. It's much better to tell her in advance. She will be more prepared, yes, but also, she will look forward to your extravagant evening every day between now and then. Women get excited by anticipation. Suspense is exhilarating for most women. She will be walking on clouds of joy for those three weeks, picking out a dress to wear, and all the time she will be thinking of you. Those three weeks will be wonderful for you, trust me. When the big night arrives, you can make her your queen, and make memories that you both can savor forever.

Do her a service – Wash her car, do the dishes, make her dinner, help renovate her parents' porch. These acts of service, big and small, let her know that you are with her in the trenches of everyday life, and that you are there for her to lean on if she ever gets exhausted or overwhelmed. Just that knowledge, that you notice and care about her needs, will give her a rush of renewed energy to finish off those pesky last chores, and hopefully to have a bit left over to embrace your love throughout the evening.

These are a few ideas. Please steal them and make good use of them. Perhaps you needed some inspiration, but I am sure you can be much more creative than me. The point is that you make a habit of thinking about what you can do to make your girl happy. A gift that comes from your heart and your creativity is more precious than something more expensive but less thoughtful. It's the thought that communicates. The actual gestures are just fun metaphors for your love. Seeing her smile is of course its own reward.

Sensual Communication

Let's take a moment to discuss sensual communication. Sensual communication is perhaps the most misunderstood and poorly mastered language there is. How do you stimulate her sexually? How do you lead her in the dance of love? It all starts with the two of you being fully comfortable with sexuality itself. You must cherish your sexual intimacy as the deepest and most divine aspect of your relationship.

Do not limit your sexual love for each other. Do not undermine it or suppress it. Celebrate it and treasure it. Of course, I am not talking about an animalistic form of love, which is predominantly an expression of savage lust. I am talking about the rich electricity that flows between you, the ever-present energy that underlies every interaction and teases you gently as you dream at night. This is what you should elevate, breathe, and communicate. Don't think that sex is sinful or something to be uncomfortable with. Sex within a committed relationship is the fruit of the tree of life, the most divine manifestation of love and life. Truly, what's left to celebrate if you can't honor and delight in each other's sexuality? What's left of a man's masculinity if his heart doesn't beat faster when he beholds his woman's beautiful body? To enjoy the glory inherent in true sexual communion, you must embrace its sanctity and divine origin.

Most people's approach to learning how to love is to study which buttons to push: the pressure points and the positions that stimulate a woman's body. There is certainly a place to study a woman's anatomy and to discover her sensitive regions, and on the right foundation, this knowledge can add to your toolbox. In and of itself however, this study is counterproductive and at best a complete waste of time. It is counterproductive because it trains your mind into believing that lovemaking is a mere physical activity, when it's in truth a cosmic energy exchange between the masculine and the feminine principles. You may show up to church with your crucifix, the Lord's prayer and the Ten Commandments memorized, but without learning how to get in touch with the cosmic energy currents, your religious experience will become stale and frozen. Lovemaking is the same way. You must learn to commune with the cosmic forces involved in the epic fusion between you and your lover. Yes, when you know this, *then* your other tools will be effective.

How do you learn to love? The place to start will surprise you; it starts with how you eat your meals. I can immediately tell someone's abilities in bed by the way they eat. Practice eating a strawberry, or your favorite fruit. Before you eat your fruit, take a moment to observe it. Look at its vibrant color and peculiar shape and feel its smooth or rugged texture. Then allow it to stimulate your emotional response as you savor its wonderful aroma. This is how you should approach your woman. Don't just jump straight to consuming her fruits. Take time to observe her vibrant colors and enticing curves, to feel her smooth texture, and to savor her delicious perfumes.

Next, take a moment to thank the universe for producing such an exquisite fruit. Whatever your religious beliefs may be, you did not bring this strawberry to existence, so be grateful for whatever forces made it happen (you would be dead without it after all.) Thank the Lord, the universe, and the cosmic forces at play to deliver you such deliciousness. Thank the farmers who nourished the soil and harvested the fruit. Visualize its journey growing from a seed to full maturity, slowly developing through the hot and cold and wet and dry seasons, nourished by natures abundant provisions. Fully appreciate the miracle involved in bringing this particular fruit in front of you. Similarly, take a moment to thank the universe for bringing this divine woman in front of you, to appreciate the miracles involved in constructing the very fabric of her existence. Be grateful for all the people who raised her, nourished her, and helped her become the individual she is today. Appreciate her journey, growing from childhood to adulthood, and recognize all the trials and hardship that helped her mature into a woman capable of giving and receiving love. Recognize the glorious symbol she represents: a true embodiment of Yin.

When you are fully present and aware of the fruit, be free to indulge. Feel its texture massage the insides of your mouth and allow its juices to converge on your tongue and permeate your entire body with its flavors. Realize that it's not just your tongue that experiences the flavor, but your entire body responds to the sensation. Take in the aroma of the fruit, let it circulate through every corner of your respiratory system. Then, when you have experienced every sensation possible from this single bite, consume it, and allow it to nourish your body and soul.

As you learn to fully experience the glory of a fruit, learning to love a woman becomes exceedingly effortless. However glorious a juicy strawberry may be, it can never compare to the magnificence of your woman. Her history, her essence, and her spirit are infinitely more potent. Her fruit is more exquisite than any other fruit. When you learn to fully experience the sanctity of the things you commune with every day, your ability to love your woman is equally magnified. When you can look at a flower with utter amazement, and allow its vibrant colors, fragrances and textures, to permeate the core of your being with joy and wonder, and when you can appreciate the spiritual wonders contained in every meal you consume, then you can bring to your lover a whole new perspective of love.

Imagine if the fruit had an awareness and a spirit. How would it feel if you consumed it with the utter amazement described above? How would it respond? Would its juices start to flow? Would it await in eager longing for you to consume it? How about if you savagely consumed it in one bite while running out the door late for your meeting? Would it experience its communion with you differently? How about your lover? Does she experience her communion differently, depending on your frame of mind? This is truly the secret to sexual fulfillment. Where you touch her and how you touch her will always be secondary to your ability to imbue her with fire and yearning. Only your presence and awareness can instill her with these feelings.

Universal Nutrition

Chapter 12

«I am the living bread that came down from Heaven. Whoever eats this bread will live forever»

~Jesus the Christ (Jn. 6:61)

E nergy is the origin of life, love, and spiritual euphoria. The dual characteristics of energy generate a binding force that draws us irresistibly together as man and woman. Understanding energy, how to attain it and how to use it, can therefore transform our lives and our relationships. Because of its paramount importance, we have dedicated much attention to it in this book. We have learned how to be aware of energy, how to control it, and how to channel it through our interactions with people. What remains is the question of how to obtain energy. This will be the subject of this final chapter. Let's take a closer look at the nature of nutrition.

Nutrition is essential. Certainly, we cannot survive without it. But what exactly do we need to nurture? Our physical bodies? Yes, indeed, but we must go beyond that. We are so much more than just our physical form, and there is so much more to our life than physical life. Jesus referenced this reality when he instructed one of his disciples to "Let the dead bury their own dead." He was implying that those without spiritual life were not alive, and that there is something more to life than just the physical functioning of this elegant machine, our fleshly body.

What is this other and essential kind of life that we must recognize, cultivate and nourish? Everyone knows that we need water and healthy food to sustain our physical body. What escapes most people is that we have other bodies that need nutrition in order to thrive. We have a spiritual body, an emotional body, and a mental body; these are at least as important as our physical selves. To reach our highest ideal as human beings we need to empower all aspects of ourselves, all our bodies, with rich and appropriate nutrition.

In this final chapter we will detail important principles of nutrition. We will discover the different forms of nourishment that come to us and learn how to carefully select the energies and elements, whether physical, emotional, mental or spiritual, that we ingest. Strengthened by the right kind of nutrition and guided by the knowledge of how to channel the resulting energies, we will be free to unleash our true latent potential. Before we talk about nutrition, however, we will take a few moments to talk about the other essential element of universal health: exercise.

Universal Exercise

Two things are necessary to obtain energy and good health: proper nutrition, and the ability to utilize it. Consider star athlete Michael Phelps, who consumes over twelve thousand calories each day (the average is about three thousand for an active male). An ordinary man consuming such amounts would certainly get very sick, very soon. However, since he channels every bit of this nutrition into swimming, his diet enables him to stand as an exceptional athlete. Food without work will make you slow and lazy, but if you work, your nutrients will empower and create you. This principle is true for all types of nutrition.

Nutrition must be channeled to serve a purpose. Otherwise it can have counteractive effects. As an illustration, electricity is intrinsically useless to us, but when channeled through a light bulb or a computer, it can change the world. If the energy is channeled in the wrong way, it can cause serious damage. Similarly, our nutrition must be channeled in order to have practical and lifegiving effects.

Spiritual and sexual energy should be transformed into creativity and love. The fire of inspiration should move us to create something beautiful, or to accomplish something worthwhile. Mental nutrition, the light of insight and understanding, should be channeled into productivity and development. Energy can be destructive if we don't utilize it to create something. For example, food on the physical plain can make us lazy, and light, which is food on the spiritual plane, can burn us if it's not channeled into a fruitful purpose. Emotional stimulation can make us hassled and clumsy, if not released through the intimate bond with our beloved. Without proper emotional discipline, it can also drive us down catastrophic trails. To develop the ability to channel nutrition, exercise and conditioning is required on every plane.

Physical Exercise

Refuse to let physical nutrition lie dormant and deter your body. Instead, convert it into energy for action. Dedicate each meal to a task at hand. Tell yourself that your breakfast will empower you to fulfill the responsibilities of the day, or to condition your body for future work. Set aside time every week to exercise and make sure every ounce of energy you consume serves a purpose. Remember that your body is your instrument to work, to play, to dance and to love, so take care of it.

Include daily exercise for strength, for cardio health, and for flexibility. Lifting weights increases your testosterone level and makes you feel powerful and confident. Cardio exercises release endorphins and make you happy, energized and focused, they improve your lungs ability to take in oxygen, and they enhance your breathing mechanics, which is of central importance to your universal health. Stretching releases tension from your body and allows your energy to flow freely. The more you train your physical body, the greater your capacity will be to accomplish great works.

Mental Exercise

A healthy mind can enrich perception with uplifted thoughts and block out disruptive thoughts. When miners dig for gold, they scan through megatons of dirt and rocks before they find that single gram of gold hidden inside that earth. If your mind is pure and well-oriented, you should be able to scan through an ocean of knowledge and information and quickly locate the gold, the central issues and necessary information. To do this you must train your mind.

Challenge yourself with intellectually stimulating activities and train your mind to control your thoughts. Practice the discipline of reining in your thoughts by teaching your wandering mind to focus. Focus on your breath, and don't allow yourself to be distracted. These exercises will enhance your ability to access the hidden powers of your mind, and to grasp essential information effectively. Every time you receive mental nutrients in the form of ideas, knowledge, or perceptions, practice putting these insights to use immediately. Create something, solve something, convey something, invent something. Don't let your knowledge lie dormant, without producing any fruits. If you realize it, or materialize it, then its meaning is enhanced by its context. Otherwise you will turn it into a shadow of its full meaning and relevance. The more you accomplish with the ideas that come to you, the more you will attract inspiring ideas and insights.

Emotional Exercise

So many people overindulge in emotional nutrition, like kids in a candy shop, and because of lack of self-control, they find themselves in a spiral of self-destruction. When we are well-fed emotionally, our love is stronger, our joy is stronger, but so is our hate, anger, jealousy, fear and lust. We have dedicated much time to self-mastery, because with self-mastery, our emotional nutrition can lead us to a true paradise, but without self-mastery, it can lead us to, well, somewhere much less fun!

To develop your emotional capacity, you must practice controlling challenging emotions. If you are easily offended, easily frustrated, or easily angered, then start by working with these weaker areas of your emotional life. If you struggle with jealousy, anger, self-pity or fear, then take time to revisit these emotions when you are ready for a challenge. Call them up, and then practice applying the insights and techniques we've studied to overcome them. Let these powerful emotions come to mind, but instead of giving in to them, focus your spirit and surrender to your breath. Allow your breath to channel your emotion through your body and to transform these currents into pure, empowering and lifegiving vibrations. Doing so will strengthen your emotional body and open the door for you to taste the riches of a transfigured emotional life.

Physical Nutrition

Now that we have gone over the subject of exercise, and how to channel nutrition, we will enter a detailed discussion of how to attain various forms of nutrients, starting with the physical. We are all aware that we must eat in order to have energy. Most of us are also aware of what kind of food is healthy and what kind we should eat only sparingly. For this reason, we will not go into too much detail regarding which foods to eat. Instead we will focus on how to eat in order to attain the greatest degree of energy. People are not generally aware of the spiritual significance of food; that it has the power to nourish our spirits, minds, and emotions as well as our physical bodies. Depending on how you eat, you may finish a meal feeling drained or feeling invigorated.

Jesus taught that our body is a sacred temple. He said, "Drink, for this is my blood; eat, for this is my body." Through this sacrament given during his last supper, Jesus gave us more than just this one specific and salvific ritual. He was also teaching us that it's possible to imbue our daily meals with meaning, and that food itself can take on great value and significance if we honor the subtler content of the fruit and bread we consume.

Think about it. If the entire cosmos was derived from a singular supreme being, doesn't that mean that each particle contains something of His essence? The primordial force is engraved within every living organism, so when we eat, we are in fact taking in a small part of the body of the almighty Creator. Consequently, we should eat consciously, express gratitude and delight, and never eat in such a way as to allow a meal to defile our spirits.

Before you start a meal, make sure your spirit is quiet and your mind is calm. Many cultures traditionally offer prayer for the food. This practice of expressing gratitude effectively helps your body anticipate and receive your meal, and it aids your mind and emotions to take in the subtler elements of the food. With proper intentions, you can absorb a spectrum of energies from your food, and find yourself peaceful, refreshed and replenished. On the other hand, as you've probably noticed, if you scarf down a plate on the run, you end up feeling more tired, nauseous and stressed, after you finish.

You can provide another important element to your meal by practicing mindfulness of purpose. As you savor the flavor and fragrance of each bite, imbue the food with your inner light and dedicate the energy it gives you to a task at hand. You might say to yourself, "I will offer this energy to give love and warmth to my sweetheart." Or, "I will be full of clarity and power to complete that essential task at work. " If you do so, you will find that you feel lighter and happier, obtain greater nutritional benefits, and that even humble food will be as tasty and invigorating as a gourmet banquet.

Another important aspect of eating is to chew properly. You have probably noticed that even while starving, your hunger is satisfied soon after you start eating, even though it takes hours to fully digest your meal. If you think about that fact, then you can appreciate the importance of chewing as part of the digestion process. This is true physically, but even more so, when you chew mindfully, subtle elements from the food are extracted. Vitality elements that would otherwise be lost in your digestion is released to your spiritual, mental and emotional bodies. Therefore, chew thoroughly, calmly, and allow your heart to savor the delightful tastes and textures of your meal.

Finally, I implore you not to overeat. Try to stop eating when you reach eighty percent of your capacity. This will leave you light and full of energy. Hunger is very important for us. When you are hungry, your body can pick up subtle particles from the air that are highly nutritious and rejuvenating for your spirit. When you are overfull or even just physically satisfied, you may notice that you are not as sensitive to what's going on around you, and your inner awareness and thinking becomes dull. Overeating inhibits the free flow of energy in your physical body, but also dulls your astral body and your ability to feel. The more you overeat, the more waste matter is stored in your body and the longer it takes to purify your system. If you understand that reality, then you can also see why fasting is valuable from a spiritual as well as a medical perspective.

<u>Fasting</u>

Undoubtedly, fasting helps us to develop the strength of will needed to sacrifice for those dear to us. Additionally, it's a highly effective method of self-purification and of cleansing and healing our blood and internal organs. Hunger gives our bodies the opportunity to become sensitive to energy that comes to us from sources other than food, such as the air, the sun, the earth, and even people. This energy is much purer than what we gain from food. Finally, fasting reminds us of how dependent we are on nature. Strong and brave as we might be, not one of us is truly independent. We are born onto and nourished by this great planet, and we need these precious resources, as well as the friendship and love offered by our social environment. Gratitude for our daily bread is a great way to keep in touch with the fact that we are indebted to this world, and that we have so much to give back if we are only mindful.

Mental Nutrition

Your mental body has an insatiable hunger for Truth. You must be alert in order to feed your mind; check behind every corner, leave no stone unturned, and ask all the questions. Constantly seek for the cosmic principles, and the primordial Truth, and your mind will become sharp and prone to enlightenment. Otherwise, if you settle for mental junk food such as biased newsfeeds, celebrity stories and cliché inspirational quotes, your mind will slowly dull. You may not notice since you will still be able to solve simple sudokus, join in the conversation with the cashier about your political viewpoint, or recall the first x number of presidents. But you may not realize that you will have lost your perception of life's wonders, of your passions, and of the fresh start provided to you free of charge at every sunrise. Mental nutrition and exercise are freely available to you through contemplation, meditation, and of course, the study of worthy writing. So, read on my curious friend.

<u>Study the Great Masters</u>

We all want to discover the Truth, and many of us are quite certain that we know it already. But the great secret that few have stumbled upon is that the Truth cannot be found in this slow and opaque physical world. What we can know here is a mere reflection of a greater Truth that can't be formulated in any human language. Therefore, when you study, open your heart and fix your gaze beyond the words and concepts, and see the spirit which underlies the written word.

I enjoy studying the teachings of great spiritual masters. I read biblical scriptures regularly, as well as the teachings of Buddha, Socrates, Confucius, and many other ancient and modern philosophers and teachers. I am particularly indebted to the teachings of Master Mikhael Aivanhov, who has taught me most of what I know about nutrition.

The great masters tried to convey their discoveries made over years of searching this world and the world beyond. These discoveries are as complex and subtle as the most rarified theories of any physicist. It's impossible to comprehend their teachings by simply reading the words and thinking about them using your intellect alone. However, if you go deeper into their meaning by reading their words with an open and inquisitive heart, reading them again and again while in meditation on the spirit underlying the words, you will glimpse other universes beyond the boundaries of this three-dimensional world.

Allow the great masters to take you beyond your comfort zone, beyond the tried and true, and beyond the thought patterns that usually get you from point a to b. There is after all an entire alphabet out there, the p's and q's, the occasional x, y or z. Take a second look and see the moonwalking bear. (Search the video to understand the reference.)

Travel and Explore

If you live your entire life in one location, it's almost impossible to avoid getting stuck in a rut of thinking the way you always have. New ideas are so few and far between that they are truly alien. The simplest, quickest and most exciting way to crack the retaining walls is to get up and discover what's out there. Once you get beyond the borders of your own little town, the unfamiliar sights and sounds reveal a world of infinite possibilities.

Every culture offers its unique flavor, however there are universal principles expressed within them all. By studying a variety of cultures with an open mind you will discover universal Truths that govern human affairs regardless of our place in this world. Whenever you meet someone from a faraway land, study them discreetly but intently. Believe that they can teach you the secrets of the universe, and in fact they will. Each culture manifests the secrets of the universe but couched in an unfamiliar language or perspective that requires you to leave your preconceived and sanitized versions behind. Each culture you embrace will provide you with new insights. It's not enough to just read a book, or to purchase an all-inclusive vacation package. Go beyond, and venture onto the narrow lanes and into the little venues with their poorly advertised "events." Mine for the riches and you won't be disappointed. When you have enough threads of understanding, you will be able to weave a fabric rich with texture and surprise, an elegant expression of your own personal Truth.

Meditation and Contemplation

Through meditation your spirit comprehends the broad unspoken realities that can be ascertained through the great teachings. As Bruce Lee might say, words are "like a finger pointing away to the moon. Don't concentrate on the finger or you will miss all that heavenly glory." The moon is the object of our gaze, not the finger. The words cannot contain the object of our curiosity and yearning. As you contemplate and meditate on these teachings, their content becomes available to you. Meditation is also a pathway to allow you to calm your thoughts. It gives rise to a peaceful state free from chatter, in which you can come into resonance with the life force coursing through your veins. You will find that meditation is an avenue to light and peace, and to a higher understanding that purify and revive.

Live a Life of Integrity

We have spoken of ways to restore and nourish the highest functions of our minds. It's worthwhile at this point, though, to mention one practice that can swiftly destroy any progress you make. This destructive habit is that of hypocrisy. Whatever you believe, say, and expect others to do must be consistent with the way you live your own life, or else your mind will lose clarity of perception. You will continuously suffer confusion because of your inner contradictions and lack of integrity.

Our failures as human beings come from two things only. One is ignorance and the other is contradiction. We end up failing or behaving wrongfully first because we don't know what is right and what is wrong. However, often we fail despite knowing what is right, because even though we know what we are supposed to do, we end up doing the opposite. An example is people who struggle with obesity and poor health. Some people do not know that a diet exclusively composed of junk food, and a lifestyle free from exercise, is detrimental to their health. Others do know this, but still choose to continue in their unhealthy habits, due to a lack of willpower. In both cases they end up destroying their bodies.

Another example is people who fail to nurture their relationships. Some people fail because they do not know what it takes to please and to nurture a woman. Others do know, but they fail to be there for her because of laziness, selfishness or resentment. To become free of these kinds of contradictions, and to bring our lives into harmony with higher ideals, we must tirelessly dedicate ourselves to the pursuit of Truth and personal integrity.

Emotional Nutrition

Most people are good at feeding themselves emotionally. Sources include soap operas, drama in their relationships, drug-induced euphoria, heated political arguments, Facebook posts gleaning affirmation and/or sympathy, and so on. The amount of emotional nutrition is not the problem in today's society, but rather the quality thereof.

An abundant supply of junk food, be it mental, physical, emotional, sexual, or spiritual, floods our environment in any modern society. There are plenty of channels to obtain this meaningless substance, free of charge. They will even feed it to you with a spoon or pour it down your throat if you aren't vigilant. We must therefore be careful of the kind of nutrition we ingest; this is perhaps especially true for emotional nutrition.

Living in isolation, without interplay with other people, is dangerous for your emotional health. Without emotional nutrition, your spirit loses vitality, and you will eventually be unable to feel compassion, love or joy. However, it's also dangerous to take in excessive amounts of low emotional contents. Don't put yourself in situations that stimulate your lower nature and push you into emotional overindulgence. Don't argue over insignificant things, stop watching trashy dramas on TV, avoid destructive relationships and so on. Instead, invest in truly life-giving relationships, primarily with your family, with your sweetheart, and with the cosmic intelligence.

Spend intimate time with your loved ones. Schedule time to share heart to heart conversations and enjoy each other's presence. Engage in stimulating and encouraging conversations. Hug often, laugh often, make love often. Be lively, emotional, and vulnerable in your interactions and you will soon see your emotional health blossom.

Spiritual Nutrition

People seek spiritual nutrition from various sources. Some seek communion with the primordial source of life, through prayer, working on their chakras, visiting nature, or reading scripture. I recommend that you engage in whichever method allows you to drink from the cosmic light. This light is the best nourishment for your soul. I'd like to share a few of my favorite methods with you here.

Nature and the Sun

The sun provides practically all the energy for our planet. Every chemical process, every movement, virtually our entire existence, is fueled by the power of the Sun. Within the rays of the sun is the purest and most pristine form of energy. For this reason, perhaps the most effective way to attain spiritual nutrition is to spend time with the sun. This is particularly true at sunrise. Certainly, the sunset is splendid, but it represents the decline, the end of life. If we want to eat well, we don't eat fruit that is deteriorating. We eat those recently picked, in their prime, fresh, and imbued with life. The sunrise symbolizes the emergence of new life, and every ray is laden with transformational spiritual and physical nutrients. Get in the habit of waking up to watch the sunrise. Meditate on the majesty of the sun and allow it to bless you with spiritual nutrition. These nutrients have the power to impart joy and meaning into your daily activities and revitalize your health and love-life.

I wish I could describe to you my brilliant encounters with the sun. The sun has cured me from many illnesses, physical, emotional, and spiritual. It has opened my spiritual senses and introduced me to a splendid wealth of love and wonder. I am thoroughly convinced that the sun contains hidden mystical treasures and nutrients science is yet to discover. There is a reason why it has been the object of worship in many ancient religions. Spend time with the sun, familiarize yourself with it, and you will soon discover what I'm talking about.

It's natural that the ideal wellspring of spiritual nutrition would be in an environment full of life. That wellspring or source is to be found in nature. Reward yourself with an occasional trip to the mountains, or the sea, or the forest. Connect with Mother Earth and experience her vibrant wildlife. Listen to the sounds, breathe in the fresh air, and connect with all that's alive. When you return, you will feel invigorated, inspired and refreshed.

Meditation

Meditation is a great tool to explore the subtler aspects of any topic. It also has the capacity to calm your mind, refresh your spirit, and imbue you with special qualities. Meditation offers intellectual nourishment along with spiritual riches. These exercises may seem obscure to you. It is strange to think how visualizations and meditation can change your circumstance, but the truth is, the quality of your life is a reflection of the elements you engage with. When we embrace powerful symbols, they can infiltrate our consciousness, and over time bear fruit in our physical conditions.

Experiment with meditating on various symbols. Consider using colors. Every color corresponds to a virtue, and if you meditate on a color, you can slowly actualize its inherent qualities. White light represents purity, but if you shine it through a prism, you realize that it harbors all the other colors. Meditate on brilliant white light, and let it permeate and energize your spirit. Imagine light all around you and use the power of visualization to make it saturate your being, heal your inner darkness, and renew your mind. This visualization can have marvelous effects if you take time for it regularly.

Music

Music is a powerful language of the spirit. Somehow, we all understand this language, even if we have never studied it. It seems that sensitivity to music is imbued in us from birth. No matter where the music is produced, what language the lyrics are in, or which instruments are played, we all seem to be able to interpret the spiritual frequencies contained in the song. Certainly, music is a key to spiritual insight.

Musical prodigies are often deeply in touch with their spirituality. That is because they have embraced a language of the spirit. Learn to see music in this way. Allow the sounds to move you and let your spirit dance in harmony with the rhythms and vibrations. Learn to play a musical instrument or take a dance class if you like. In any case, the mechanics of the production of music is less important than your ability to let it nurture and awaken your spirit.

Be mindful of the music you listen to. Some music speaks to the lower factions of your spirit, and will make you angry, depressed or cynical. Music is such a powerful tool, so be aware of the effect that your musical library has on your soul. Don't let it tear you apart or push you to indulge in thoughts and emotions rising from your lower nature. Instead, listen to music that inspires you, and imbues you with sensations of joy, excitement, and true love. This is true for any kind of art. Be therefore mindful of the types of art you indulge in. The arts touch your soul, and their impact resonates throughout the mental, spiritual, emotional and even physical aspects of yourself.

Breathing

Your breath is perhaps the most important tool to obtain nutrition, as well as to distribute energy throughout your body. Scientists are only starting to realize this, but yogis have known this truth for centuries. As you breathe, you take in myriads of subtle particles, minerals and chemicals from the air. This nourishes your body, as well as your spirit and mind. Healthy breathing can purify your system and fuel you with the life force, improper breathing can poison your system and make you sick.

Whenever you take in nutrition, remember to breathe. When you eat, breathe, when you study, breathe, when you make love, breathe. Very often, we forget to breathe when we consume nutrients, and we thus fail to fully absorb the elements we are engaging with.

Taking a course in Yoga or Thai Chi will teach you proper breathing techniques much more effectively than I can through this book. The greatest inhibitor to proper breathing, however, is that we forget, so catch yourself and remember to breathe. Breathe slowly, deeply and consciously. Breathe in through your nose and fill your lungs with healing oxygen, then hold it in for a moment before exhaling slowly, unforcedly, and consciously through your nose. Allow your body and soul to filter out all the nutrients it needs before expelling what it doesn't need. Every breath of air becomes part of the process of purification and healing.

The breath is not only a tool to take in nutrition, it's also a tool to distribute energy throughout your body. Energy tends to get stuck in different places in your body due to emotional constrictions, sexual impurity or mental stress, primarily in your chest, abdomen and genitals. This unnatural tension is detrimental to your health. Proper breathing can help you distribute beneficial energies and release harmful ones. This is an effective method to overcome internal problems and to free your energy to pass unhindered through your body. Whenever you feel tired, stressed and drained, return to the practice of deep breathing. Allow it to release muscular tensions, purify your mental environment, awaken your spirit, and heal your inner conflicts.

Sexual Nutrition

When the masculine and the feminine principle coalesce, the cosmic force of creation begins. This unity contains the greatest potential for spiritual and emotional nutrition. To actualize these nutrients, and obtain the towering heights of sexual fulfillment, we must understand the symbolism inherent to the Yin & Yang dynamic.

Consider the extraordinary nature of the masculine and feminine unity as expressed in nature. When the electron and the proton coalesce, their creative harmony can create anything from a delicious passion fruit to the towering Great Wall of China. Based on the four-position-foundation, a man and a woman have the power to create the most precious element in the universe, the fifth element, that of life. The creative harmony of the masculine and feminine principle provides infinite possibilities.

What started this great universe? What was the Big Bang? What was the Great Light? What was powerful enough to create a universe over 8 septillion (8.8×10^{23}) kilometers wide, including over a sextillion (10^{21}) stars, and more than one hundred and seventy billion galaxies, and that keeps expanding today after over twelve billion years? The answer can be nothing less than a supernatural climax between Yin & Yang. According to the book of Genesis, God created man *and* woman in His image. In agreement with ancient Greek and Chinese philosophy, it is not the masculine or the feminine that represent the Creator, but rather the fusion of these cosmic principles. Therefor their union is inherent in everything we know.

In light of these discoveries, we must reevaluate our understanding of sexuality, and begin to see it in connection to a cosmic phenomenon inherent to the creative and founding force of our universe. Sexual love is the supreme expression of the love of the Creator and embodies the very purpose of life. Keeping this understanding in mind allows us to reach high and dig deep when we explore the potential of our sexual union. Instead of limiting ourselves to mere physical stimulation, we can embrace sexuality as an expression of the life force itself. We can then realize the deep spiritual significance of our union, and reach a oneness that fuses our thoughts, our emotions, our sensations and our breaths.

There are many methods for developing and training your sexual capacity, and of course, some are more elevated than others. Go back and review our many discussions on this subject throughout the book for inspiration but use your own experience to uncover a personal understanding. With dedication and meditation, you will find the right path for you. What matters is that you have an ideal in mind and don't settle for less. When you attain a state of life-giving sexual union with your sweetheart, it will replenish you both and fill you with uncharted levels of inspiration and passion.

Mysteries of Yin

Traveling around the world has finally brought me full circle, physically and philosophically. I discovered that the fulfillment of life's purpose is found in a woman's loving embrace. Within her lays the keys to supreme fulfillment, the second great blessing, and the source of the most pristine universal nutrients.

This communion is our source of emotional nutrition as we grow in intimacy, our source of mental nutrition as we resolve trials and obstacles, our source of physical nutrition as we strive to provide, and our source of sexual and spiritual energy as we grow in our love. She is a part of a cosmic principle, and through our oneness with her, we can actualize the life force that permeate and control every interaction in our universe. By dedicating ourselves fully to Yin, as expressed through our own girl, we can enjoy the most satisfying nutrients, the tastiest joys, and the sweetest pleasures.

Our relationships can be our most euphoric source of inspiration, passion, and joy, but inherent to this bond is sacrifice and trust. Many people consider their relationships a 50/50 contract, hoping they will reap 100% of the benefits. But to obtain our supreme potential we must devote ourselves wholeheartedly. When parents have their child in mind, they don't count the favors they have done for him or her. They never keep a record of all the times they went without sleep or of how much money they spent on shoes, food, or school supplies. Parents continue to give, they forget what they gave, and then give still more. After they've given everything, they are left with regret because they couldn't give more. They do this because their child is more precious to them than anything in the world. In order to taste the depths and heights of true love and true life, we must extend this same fervent devotion to our beloved.

The paradoxical truth is that the more you give, the more comes back to you. This is the circle of life. Partly because people will express gratitude, return your affections, and imitate your sacrifice, but beyond human dynamics, there are subtle energies that you receive when you go beyond your limitations and offer loving care to another. Everything you do to the benefit of others fuels your cells with rich vitality elements. These subtle particles are related to the origin of life and are a part of the quintessential energy that sustain our universe. This force of life makes the difference between duty and vocation, between lust and passion, between a house and home, and between having only the name of being alive vs sharing eternal life and eternal love with your beloved.

The pursuit of the ideal is not free of hardships. It will push you to the edge of your comfort zone, force you to dive into the wisdom of the ages, and fully devote yourself. With persistence, however, you will tap into hidden resources that lights up your path. As you exercise the principles detailed in this book, as well as the ones you learn along your journey and continuous study, you will progressively uncover deeper layers of truth, and grow deeper in intimacy with your beloved. Ultimately, as time progresses, and you reach new levels of maturity and wisdom, you will find the hidden treasures contained in the *Mysteries of Yin*.

The End

ABOUT THE AUTHOR

J.S. Lea is a global citizen, husband, father, scientist, philosopher, life-coach, adventurer, and ardent student of the secrets of the universe. Originally from Norway, he lives with his wife and daughter in Fort Worth, Texas, and combines his work as a mechanical engineer with studying and teaching the principles of marital harmony. After multiple life-changing experiences in his global ventures, and several profound encounters with the spiritual world, he believes to be called by the cosmic intelligence to share his experiences and insights about relationships. He believes that the perfect union between a man and a woman holds the key to true happiness, individual perfection, and world redemption.

Connect with the Author

Want to hear more? To continue the conversations and hear more stories and insights from Mysteries of Yin, connect with the author through his social media platform
Facebook.com/jsleaauthor

Enjoyed this book?

Please share your review, so it may reach others.

www.ingramcontent.com/pod-product-compliance
Lightning Source LLC
Chambersburg PA
CBHW031510270326

41930CB00006B/345

9781733368506